Angel Wings

He shall cover thee with his feathers, and under his wings shalt thou trust; his truth shall be thy shield and buckler. Ps. 91:4 [KJV]

JANET PHIPPS LESTER

Copyright © 2014 Janet Phipps Lester
All rights reserved.

ISBN: 1497594480
ISBN 13: 9781497594487

Table of Contents

Dedication	v
Acknowledgments	vii
A Journey of Faith	1
Lisa	7
Honeysuckle and Moonlight	11
A Gift of Love	17
House in the Clearing	19
Lantern in the Morning	25
Meggy May	31
Broth and Jello	37
Gladys	43
Jilli	47
Melissa	49
Ruben	59
Scotty	67
Teensy	73
The Sweater	79
The Letter Jacket	85
Messengers	89
Mountain Path	95
Dad's Discipline	99
The Soup Bean Kettle	105
The Taxi	109

The Vision	113
Watermelon	115
White Star Café	117
Words Do Hurt	121
Mother's Bucket List	127
Blackberries and Buttermilk	133
The Dream	137

Dedication

Those who bring sunshine to the lives of others cannot keep it from themselves --- James Barrie.

This book is dedicated to my five grandchildren: Sara, Morgan, Emily, Matthew and Brooke. They are my earth angels and like rays of sunshine, they warm my heart.

My grandchildren have beautiful differences. Sara has a keen intellect and a photographic memory. Emily and Morgan have a natural ability to work with children. Both are in college studying for degrees in early childhood education. My grandson, Matthew is a talented athlete and plans to enter the medical field. Brooke, the youngest grandchild, is an accomplished artist and wants to attend an art institute to study design. The cousins love each other and have fun when they get together.

Here are two smile makers involving two of my grandchildren.

Morgan and her father were in line to see Santa Claus. Morgan was two years old and the closer she got to this man with the long white beard, the more hesitant she became.
As her turn neared, Morgan decided that she was not going to leave her father and sit on Santa's lap.

"I wanna go home now. I don't want to talk to Santa Claus. No! No! No!"

"Morgan, if you don't tell Santa what you want for Christmas, how will he know?" asked her father.

Morgan responded, "Call him on the phone."

Number two involves my granddaughter, Sara Beth.

Three-year old Sara Beth sashayed down the aisle of the grocery store with her grandmother, whom she calls Mimi. Sara Beth loved to shop and there were always several interesting items in the cart at the checkout counter.

As Mimi concentrated on her shopping, she suddenly realized Sara Beth was no longer with her. She panicked and called her name. No answer. In the next aisle, she heard a commotion. People were saying, "No, no, no! Don't do that?'

Mimi ran to the next aisle and there to her relief, in the middle of the pet food aisle, was her granddaughter. Her relief quickly turned to shock when she noticed Sara Beth's jeans and underpants laying on the floor and her little bare butt sitting on a dog food bowl.

"Mimi, pee, pee in the potty," Sara Beth proudly exclaimed as she clapped her hands.

Sara Beth did not like the unhappy look on her Mimi's face. The family always clapped their hands and jumped up and down when she tinkled in the potty. Why was her Mimi upset?

"This is a dog bowl, Sara Beth. You put food in it for a dog. You do not pee in it."

Embarrassed, Mimi quickly dressed her granddaughter and picked up the bowl. She hurried to the back of the store in search of a rest room to empty the tinkle. She was perplexed as to what to do with the bowl.

At the checkout counter, Sara Beth looks up at her Mimi with big brown innocent eyes and asks, "Mimi, why are you buying a dog bowl? You don't have a dog."

Acknowledgments

Special thanks go to my Writers' Guild for their insight and suggestions for several of the stories in this book.

Thank to Caleb Humphries at Computer Depot for answering so many of my computer questions with such patience.

Thanks to my family for letting me write stories about them, to former students and other dear people who shared their stories with me and allowed me to include them in this book. Stories written in the first person are experiences from the author's life.

While the stories are all based on true events, some names and other details have been changed for privacy. Conversations in the stories of a time long gone were written as they might have occurred.

A Journey of Faith

God has resources we know nothing about, solutions outside our reality, provisions outside our possibility. --- Max Lucado

A ringing phone shattered the silence in a house enveloped in sadness on that rainy Sunday morning in February, 1974.

"Can you come and pick me up? The doctor has released me from the hospital and I want to go home," came the melancholy voice over the phone.

"Mother, I don't have enough gas in the car to get there. It's Sunday and the stations are closed," I said sadly.

"I'll just have to stay here another day. I know you would come if you could."

I hung up the phone, and helplessness and frustration tore at me. My mother needed me, and I couldn't help her. The pain of knowing she was alone in her grief was painful. I pictured my mother sitting alone in her impersonal hospital room, her eyes dark with pain, her head bowed in grief and no one in the family with her.

My sixty-year-old father had been buried a few days earlier following death from a massive heart attack. Mother hospitalized at the time for disc problems in her back and bleeding stomach ulcers was released from the hospital only long enough for my father's funeral. She was readmitted to the hospital the following day for more tests and treatment.

Even though mother's physical problems were improved enough to go home, I knew her emotional state was fragile with the unexpected loss of my dad. Worry about my mother and grief from the loss of my father weighed heavily on me. I feared the vulnerable state of Mother's physical and emotional health could push her deeper into the pit of the depression she had suffered for many years.

My husband and I lived with our two children in a small town nestled in a valley at the foot of a mountain range. My mother was in a hospital eighty miles away. At the time, the gasoline shortage made travel difficult. The lines were long and most stations only allowed two gallons per car.

"Sorry, we're out. Come back tomorrow," were the dreaded words no one wanted to hear.

"Mother is alone, she needs me and I'm going to her." I told my husband

"You don't have enough gas in the car to get to the hospital. If you get stranded, I can't come to get you. How are you going to get back home? Be reasonable. Please don't do this," my husband pleaded.

His words were logical, but my decision remained firm! I threw on a sweatshirt and jeans then checked my purse for money. Twenty dollars – that ought to be enough. With no banks open on Sunday, it would have to do. As I shut the car door, my husband's frustrated voice followed me from the doorway.

"I'll be able to find fuel along the way," I called to him as I pulled out of the driveway. I kept praying over and over again, "Please, God, let me get to my mother."

Twenty miles from the hospital, the gas hand registered empty. All of the gasoline stations along the way had signs saying,

"Closed. No Gas." I knew I was in deep trouble. My search for fuel had proved fruitless.

Pulling my car over on the shoulder of the highway near a business that my husband and I patronized, I put my head down on the steering wheel and breathed a sigh of desperation, "Oh, Lord! What a mess I've gotten myself into. What am I going to do?" I said aloud. Tears of despair streamed down my face.

I raised my head and across the highway on a knoll stood a small white wood building with two gas pumps in front. The pumps were rounded on top not like the modern square ones. I hadn't noticed the place when I pulled off the road. With a glimmer of hope, I dried my eyes and drove my car across the highway and up the narrow incline to what appeared to be a gas station. Was there enough gas in the car to make it to the pumps? My heart dropped; there were no cars. If the place was open and had available gasoline, there would be a line of cars.

Before I could make plans for my next step, a man of small stature wearing a brown leather newsboy's cap came through the door of the small white building.

"Your business is open? Do you have any gasoline?" I called out with hopeful anticipation in my voice.

"Yes, we do. How much do you want?" he asked with a twinkle in his eye.

"You do! You have gasoline! How much can I have?" I asked hesitantly but with mounting excitement.

"All you want," he answered.

All I wanted! I could not believe my ears! This sweet man was giving me a full tank. It had been weeks since our old green car had sported a full tank.

"Thank you, Lord, thank you, thank you!" I prayed.

It did seem odd that there were no other cars, but my focus was getting to my mother so I didn't really spend time chasing that thought.

I began to worry if I had enough money, but the pump stopped at exactly twenty dollars! What luck! I paid the man, thanked him profusely and was happily on my way.

"Mother will be surprised. She's not expecting me until tomorrow," I said aloud to myself as I traveled down the highway. Arriving at the hospital, the first thing I did was telephone my husband from the pay phone in the lobby. He was relieved that I had arrived safely but was full of questions about how I'd managed to get a full tank of gasoline.

"It's true! It is really true! Can you believe it? My gas tank is full and I can hardly wait to surprise Mother. I'll tell you all about it later." I hung up the phone and headed for my mother's room.

When I arrived at her hospital room, she was happy to see me but did not seem surprised. I was somewhat puzzled by her reaction.

"Mother, I have a full tank of gasoline, a full tank. That hasn't happened in I don't know how long. By the way, you don't seem surprised that I'm here."

"I knew you would come. I've already filled out all my paperwork and I'm ready to leave. I've been sitting her waiting for you. I've been praying since I talked to you on the phone. I believed that some way God would get you here. He did. Let's go home," my mother said with relief in her voice.

I admired my mother's faith, and wished I could be like more like her. She encouraged me often by telling me, "God loves us all, but He has favorites that He scatters about the world, only they don't know they're special. You are one of those people," she would say. I would smile and think—spoken just like a mother. It was not me that was special, it was her.

When Mother sat down, her Bible was never far from her side. She had a great love for and faith in God, and she was always helping others.

As we left the hospital Mother said, "Take me to my home, not yours. I have to face that house without your dad in it and I want to get that painful task over with as soon as possible."

There was no convincing her to come and visit with my family for a few days. Going to her own home would be the first in a long series of painful steps for my mother in facing life without my father.

After driving the hundred miles or so from the hospital to her home and getting her through an emotional homecoming, she was ready for a rest. I ached for her because I knew climbing into the bed she had shared with my dad for forty years would be difficult.

Mother tried unsuccessfully to hide her pain from me. She encouraged me to go on home to my own family. Although I was hesitant to leave, my grandparents assured me they would take good care of her.

I traveled the fifty miles or so to my home and pondered the events of the day. When I pulled the car into my driveway later that night, the gasoline hand registered empty.

"Thank you, Lord, for what you did for my family today and blessings on the man at the gas station who gave me the fuel to accomplish what I needed to do," I prayed aloud.

Several weeks later, we were able to get enough fuel to travel to the gas station to thank the man and tell him what that tank of gasoline meant to us. It had been the major topic of conversation in my family for weeks.

When we reached the place where the white wood building was supposed to be, it was not there. The lane leading up to the knoll was not there either.

I didn't understand. There was a gas station here. It can't have just disappeared. There was once a television program called The Twilight Zone. I felt like I was in the twilight zone. There was nothing normal about this situation.

The knoll was an empty field with tall brown grass blowing in the breeze. There were no gas pumps, no white building and no little man in a newsboy's cap.

Later when I related these unexplainable events to my mother, she said, "You met an angel!"

Every time I drive by that area, I marvel at God's goodness. I don't know if it was an angel that helped me that day, but I do know God tells us that He is a present help in times of trouble. At a moment of need for my family, God answered our prayers and gave us a miracle. I got a full tank of gasoline in a time when it was so scarce that a friend siphoned gas from his truck into our car so we could attend my dad's funeral.

Paul recorded Jesus words, "My grace is sufficient for thee; for strength is made perfect in weakness." II Corinthians 12:9 [KJV]

Mother lives in heaven now but her faith still lives on in the hearts of her loved ones left behind.

Lisa

Before you were conceived, I wanted you
Before you were born I loved you
Before you were here an hour, I would die for you
This is the miracle of Life. --- Maureen Hawkins

Lisa yearned for a baby. Her husband was compassionate but found it difficult to understand the soul-searing pain of empty arms for a woman who yearns for a child. Nothing but a baby can satisfy that desperate need. It is difficult to understand unless you have been there and experienced the pain.

Many times her disappointment was so great Lisa would roll into a fetal position and cry until she was so exhausted she slept. She even found herself resentful of any pregnant woman she saw whether or not she knew the person.

Her doctor tried, but was unable to help her, and recommended she and her husband see a fertility specialist. The fertility treatments the specialist recommended did nothing but drain their financial resources. Faithfully taking the fertility drugs and all the procedures suggested brought no success. The doctor asked Lisa to go for some tests.

Following the tests, he called her to his office, and the news was not good. A tumor was found on an ovary; the tumor was solid and that was cause for concern. The doctor recommended immediate surgery. If the tumor proved to be malignant, he would do a hysterectomy while she was sedated.

Lisa and her family were devastated by the news. On the day of surgery, the prayerful family tried to be positive but fear was written on everybody's face. The doctor said he would call when he had news. The frightened young woman went into surgery not knowing whether she would come out with her reproductive organs intact or gone, along with her hope for children.

Finally, in what seemed like an eternity, the phone rang in the waiting room. Lisa's husband picked up the phone to learn from the doctor there was no malignancy, and the tumor had been removed. There were tears of joy that the tumor was benign. There would be no hysterectomy, and the hope for children was still alive.

The family thanked God for answered prayers. After Lisa's recovery, her mother asked her to visit a sweet spirited black woman she had recently met.

"Mrs. Sadie is one the most compassionate Christian women I have ever met and I want her to pray for you."

Lisa believed in the power of prayer.

Mrs. Sadie invited Lisa and her mother to her home. When they arrived, she ushered them in to her warm, cozy living room. She prayed a beautiful prayer and anointed the young woman on her forehead with a bit of oil she took from a tiny vial.

"On Sunday I'll request my church family to pray that you will conceive a child," Ms. Sadie assured the hopeful young woman. "Lisa, nothing is impossible with God."

Lisa was greatly moved by the caring woman's faith which strengthened her own. She stopped all her fertility treatments and relied on her faith that God would answer her prayers. One year later the happy mother gave birth to a beautiful daughter with blonde hair and blue eyes. Two years later came a golden-haired son.

But without faith it is impossible to please him for he that cometh to God must believe that he is, and that he is a rewarder of them that diligently seek him. [KJV]

Honeysuckle and Moonlight

Come, Fairies, take me out of this dull world, for I would ride upon the wind and dance upon the mountains like a flame! --- John Keats

A million stars and a full moon painted the little cabin in silvery light. The smell of honeysuckle permeated the night air, and the insects' droning concert was punctuated ever so often with the scream of a distant wildcat or the nearby hoot of an owl.

Molly, lost in her thoughts, sat on the porch steps barely noticing the sweet summer night. A shapeless homespun dress, limp and dirty from long hours of hoeing corn, hung about her sturdy body. Her braids tied with bits of string could not contain the wisps of hair that were freeing themselves and framing her round plump face.

"Trapper, when I wake up in the morning I'll be sixteen, and I'll be hoeing corn all day. Don't sound like a fun birthday does it, boy," Molly sighed as she made her way to the cabin door. Trapper gave her a dripping lick as an answer. Molly gave him a rub behind his ears, left him on the porch and headed for bed.

Far away at the foot of the mountain, Molly heard the faint sound of a train whistle. The lonely sound always gave her a melancholy feeling. She thought about those people on the train and wondered what it would be like to ride a train and see different places. She loved her family but at times this mountain was a lonely place. The isolated cabin could be reached only on foot or horse back. The trek up the mountain from the big road was an arduous one so company was rare.

"Time to get up! Chores to be done before we eat," Mommy called.

Molly had fallen asleep as soon as her head hit the pillow. It seemed as if she had just gone to bed and now Mommy was calling them to get up. Molly and her three sisters slept on two corn shuck mattresses in one corner of the cabin; the four boys slept in the loft. Mommy and Pa slept in a little room hooked onto the front of the cabin.

A huge fireplace with black pots, long handled skillets, and fireplace implements hanging from hooks covered the other end of the cabin. After wishing Molly a happy birthday, the family sat down to a breakfast of fried crisp fat back, eggs, gravy, corn pone and homemade syrup.

"Molly, you been moping around for days. What's wrong, child?" Mommy asked as they were cleaning up after the morning meal.

"Mommy, why do you reckon John Ed won't talk to me?" Molly asked sadly.

"Child, are you and John Ed sweet on each other?"

"I'm sweet on him but he ain't sweet on me. I wish he was. Mommy, John Ed don't know it, but he's going to marry me someday," Molly said with determination.

"Now, Molly, I believe God means for his children to go down life's way two by two but not one dragging the other one. You wait 'til after John Ed gets nerve enough to ask your pa to let him come courting, then you can get your hopes up," said Mommy with a grin.

"Joe says he thinks John Ed likes me some. Every time he comes to go hunting with Joe, he looks at me and grins, but he won't talk," said Molly as she helped her Mommy get the noon meal packed up.

"Child, John Ed's too shy to marry anybody. You're a mite bossy and I thank you scare John Ed." Mommy said with a grin.

"It's time to get going," called Pa from the cabin door.

The family made their way to the fields and began their long day of hoeing corn in the hot sun. Pa raised a lot of corn not only to feed the family but the farm animals as well.

There was a short break to eat their noon meal of corn pone, fried crisp fat back left from breakfast, green onions from the garden and cold buttermilk Mommy had cooling in the creek. It was nice to rest and picnic with her family under the cool shade of an apple tree at the edge of the cornfield.

Molly could barely keep her eyes open as she lay on the soft ground under the tree. She was dozing off when Pa called them back to work.

When the day ended and they were trudging home Joe spoke up, "Why, there comes John Ed on his horse." Joe looked over and winked at his sister.

"Hey, John Ed, come on up to the house and eat supper with us. It's Molly's birthday." Joe said grinning sheepishly.

Molly glared at Joe as she looked down at her rumpled dress and tried to tuck her unruly hair into her braids. She turned and ran to the cabin to wash off some of the sweat and grime before the others got there.

Supper was creasy greens, a hobby of corn pone, a platter of fried green tomatoes, big slabs of salt cured ham, fried potatoes with onions, a bowl of fresh churned butter, buttermilk, and blackberry cobbler for dessert.

With the fragrance of honeysuckle coming through the open cabin door and John Ed right across the table, Molly thought this was turning out to be a pretty good birthday after all.

During Pa's blessing, Molly lifted her eyes and studied this boy she wanted to marry someday. His work clothes were clean but patched and worn, and he wore no shoes. Hardly anybody on the mountain wore shoes except in the winter. Molly wished John Ed would raise his eyes and look in her direction but he never did.

After supper was over Mommy handed the children some pennies, "You all can play crack-a-do. See who can toss the penny closest to that crack in the floor." Her family watched the game while Molly sneaked glances at John Ed as they sat before the fireplace.

All the attention Molly was giving John Ed was making him uncomfortable.

"Well, Miz Elly, it was a right good supper! Since me and Joe ain't going coon hunting tonight, I'll be gitting on home fore its full dark." said John Ed, as he made his way to the cabin door.

"Me and Trapper'll walk with you to get your horse, John Ed," volunteered Molly. She loved being in the moonlight with John Ed and the smell of honeysuckle all around them.

John Ed felt uneasy the way Molly was looking at him! As they walked across the yard and down by the barn to untie John Ed's horse, Molly said, "Uh, John Ed, you ever thought about getting married someday?"

"No, I ain't," said John Ed emphatically as he jerked his head in surprise toward Molly.

"Don't get in a huff, John Ed. I said someday, not right now! Anybody you'd like to marry, if you did think about it?"

John Ed didn't answer, as he swung himself onto his horse. Lately John Ed had thought a lot about Molly. People their age did marry. If he could get a job with the lumber company over on Lick Creek, maybe he'd ask Molly to marry him. After all they were both sixteen and he did like her.

"I ain't never seen nobody take off so fast." Molly said to Trapper as she watched the horse and rider disappear into the woods.

As she and the dog walked back to the cabin, Molly was regretting her impulsive words about getting married, "Well, Trapper, I guess I scared him off for good this time, but it don't matter cause I ain't never speaking to him again."

Weeks passed and although John Ed visited occasionally to go hunting or fishing with her brothers, Molly was too stubborn to talk to him. He wanted to talk to her, but he was too shy. John Ed thought she was pretty but bossy and strong willed. He lied to her when he said he had not thought about getting married. He liked Molly a lot but he was scared of her.

One crisp fall day, Molly was helping her mommy do the wash down by the creek when she saw John Ed come trotting along the creek bank on his horse. He got down from his horse and walked over to Molly with determination and courage and blurted out, "I got me a job over at Lick Creek with the lumber company and I reckon . . ."

"You reckon what, John Ed?" She was still plenty mad at him, but Molly was glad to have a break from the washboard. Her knuckles were beginning to bleed.

"I reckon . . . . I reckon . . ." His face was red and John Ed couldn't seem to get out his words.

"You want to tell me something, John Ed?"

Fear was evident in John Ed's voice but he plunged ahead, "I already talked to your pa and he said it was all right with him; it was up to you."

"What's up to me, John Ed?"

"Molly, me and you, we're sixteen. You like me, don't you?"

"John Ed, you want to come courting me?"

'Yeah, but I . . uh . .uh. . I want us to get married."

"Oh, you do, do you? Now you want to marry me. Well, John Ed, don't do me no favors; you jumped on your horse and took off like a scared haint last time I mentioned marrying."

Molly was too stubborn to let him see how excited she was. She couldn't believe what she was hearing.

"Yeah, I am sorry about running out on you that night, Molly. I don't know what come over me."

John Ed kept on talking. He knew if he stopped, he would never say what he came to say.

"Molly, there's a circuit riding preacher coming through three weeks from Sunday. Is it alright with you if we get married on horseback over in the big road and then ride on down to Lick Creek? There's a boarding house there where we can stay 'til we find us a place." John Ed was relieved to get out what he wanted to say. It had taken all the courage he could muster and the look on Molly's face scared him to death.

"John Ed, you ain't hardly said more than two words to me in your whole life and you're asking me to marry you. You ain't even come courting me; you beat all, you know that, John Ed." Molly said with all the emotion she could muster.

Molly turned and started walking back up the hill toward the cabin with Trapper at her bare heels. She looked back and smiled to herself as John Ed and her mommy were staring after her with their mouths wide open.

"John Ed, don't you fret now," said Ms. Elly. "She'll come around. I know she's sweet on you but ain't you all a mite young to be marrying?"

"Miz Elly, I know we ain't but sixteen, but my ma married my pa when she was fifteen. I got me a job and I want to take Molly with me. Is it all right with you?"

"Well, I guess so. Come on up to the house, John Ed; we got a lot to talk about."

I'll just let John Ed sweat for a while, but not too long thought Molly, as she bounced up the hill with lightness in her step. She wondered what it would be like to kiss John Ed; she felt her face grow hot.

"I dearly do like that boy," she said as she glanced upward to thank God for answering her prayer. "Life is good, ain't it, Trapper."

A Gift of Love

"Christmas is doing a little something extra for someone."---Charles Schutz

Christmas wrappings covered the floor as our family excitedly opened their treasures. Our two children could barely contain their excitement as each present opened brought squeals of delight.

My husband and I relaxed with cups of wassail while watching our seven-year old son, Mark, and nine-year old daughter, Lisa, tear into their surprises.

Red bows, holly with red berries and lots of snow-sprayed greenery transformed the house into a winter wonderland. Red and green are my favorite colors for Christmas. The new mauves and pinks are not Christmas colors to me.

The tree twinkled with colored lights, and candles lit all the windowsills. The delicious aroma of Christmas goodies wafted through the house, and the fire in the fireplace seemed to dance to the music softly playing in the background.

Surveying the scene before me, I bowed my head to thank God for my family and the love we shared when I felt a soft touch on my shoulder. I lifted my head and opened my eyes to see my son, Mark, handing me a present he had wrapped himself.

"Mommy, this is for you," said Mark with excitement shinning in his big brown eyes.

"Thank you, honey."

The rectangular box was wrapped seven-year old style with paper folded and bunched at the ends and taped here and there. I opened the box and an unusual looking object fell out.

The object was oblong and covered in fur. Not wanting to hurt Mark's feelings by asking what the object was supposed to be, I said with enthusiasm, "Mark, tell me about this creative gift. I love it."

"See, Mommy," said Mark, it's a rabbit's foot, and it'll bring you good luck. I made it myself so a rabbit didn't have to lose its foot. I pulled fur from your coat in the closet, but I got it from the inside where it won't show."

The fur Mark pulled from an old mouton coat in my closet glued onto a paw-shaped part from one of his toys did resemble a rabbit's foot. In fact, it was quite creative.

"I love it, Mark. My very own rabbit's foot; I'll treasure it always." My eyes became misty as I hugged Mark knowing the creativity and love he'd put into this gift for me.

Mark is now a grown man with a family of his own and I'm a little old lady. But I remembers that wonderful, happy Christmas when I received one of my all-time favorite gifts – a "rabbit's foot."

House in the Clearing

A woman when she is in travail hath sorrow, because her hour is come: but as soon as she is delivered of the child, she remembereth no more the anguish, for joy that a man is born into the world. John 16:21[KJV]

Four-year old Gail lay in the porch swing with one leg on the floor pushing the swing back and forth. The sun was shining and the birds singing like any other summer day but something strange was going on in the house. Gail was scared. She could hear her mother moaning and sometimes even screaming. Her daddy was acting funny, too. He sent her outside and wouldn't let her stay with her mommy.

Gail's grandma came huffing up the path to the house. She lived half a mile away and didn't come to visit this early in the morning. She barely acknowledged Gail as she rushed through the screen door. Now her grandma was acting funny.

"I'm going for the doctor," said her father rushing out the door and into his old pickup truck parked in the yard.

"We don't need the doctor. A doctor is too expensive; a midwife will do. I'll send your pop for the one that delivered Gail," called Jim's mother with annoyance in her voice.

"Mother, that old woman is over eighty-five years old, and she's not that clean. I'm going for the doctor. I will not sacrifice the safety of my wife and your grandchild to save money."

Jim recognized that his mother was bossy and he usually ended up doing her bidding, but not this time. His wife had asked for a doctor and he wanted to make that happen.

The nearest doctor lived in town eight miles away. Jim's old pickup truck sputtered and bounced down the grassy path from the house toward the road leading into town. Worry and fear weighed so heavy on him that he could barely breathe. Could he get the doctor and be home in time? Would the doctor be there, or would he be out in the mountain somewhere with another patient? All this was running through his mind as his old truck rattled over the rocky narrow dirt road toward town.

Gail wondered why her daddy was going into town for the doctor. Something bad must be wrong with her mother. Gail lay in the swing and cried; she wanted her mommy, but her grandma would not let her in the house.

Grandma opened the screen door and walked over to Gail. "Stop crying. Your mother is going to be all right; she is getting ready for the stork. Soon you will have a little baby brother or sister then you can see your mommy. In the meantime be looking for a big white bird to come down out of the sky. They are called storks and they bring babies. Its beak will be holding a blanket with your baby sister or brother inside."

"Grandma, I want to see my mommy."

"Not now," her grandma said as she turned to go.

Later the pickup truck pulled into the yard. The doctor emerged carrying a black bag, his expression somber as he entered the house. Going immediately to his patient's bedside, he removed his coat, rolled up his sleeves and asked for hot water, soap and clean towels.

Dora's blue eyes were dark with pain and her long black hair spread on the pillow accentuated the paleness of her skin. The doctor studied this young mother whom he had known from a child. He knew her to be a lovely young woman both in character and appearance.

"I'm glad you are here," said Dora with relief in her voice. She studied this man who came to help her. He stood over six feet tall with a thick mop of gray hair falling over his forehead as he bent to examine her. His glasses slid down his nose and Dora noticed his eyes held a stern serious look which belied his caring nature.

This doctor being the only medical man within fifty miles did his best to care for hurting people often riding his horse through the snow and rain into areas where his car could not travel.

Jim didn't go inside with the doctor rather he traipsed around the house where the men who came with their wives to join in the excitement of a birth were talking, smoking cigarettes and chewing tobacco. The expectant father paced back and forth from the back yard to the front smoking one cigarette after another. His hair was sticking up where he kept running his fingers through it. One side of his shirt was hanging out of his trousers; the other side was bunched up against his suspenders. Every time his wife cried out, the frazzled husband put his head against the side of the house and tears rolled down his face. Gail cried, too. Once when Dora's mother screamed several times close together, Jim vomited in the grass.

Gail was frantic. Her mommy was screaming, her daddy was throwing up and there was no big bird coming out of the sky. She went back to the swing and started swinging again. Her world had gone crazy and she wanted her mommy. She wanted to sit on her mother's lap and play with her hair. She had noticed lately her mother's belly was so fat it took up all her lap.

The recently built white house where the young family lived stood in a clearing surrounded by woodlands and mountains. The house consisted of a kitchen, a bedroom and a room the family called the front room where Dora lay. This large room contained a bed, several rocking chairs, small tables with lamps, Gail's crib, and a fireplace for warmth. This morning the gray tin roof glistened in the sunlight, and a gentle breeze coming through the windows brought the smell of fresh air mingled with the smell of new lumber.

The house had three sparsely but adequately furnished rooms that were neat and well kept. Electricity, newly installed, brought a cheery light to the small home. The light came from a single globe screwed into an electric cord hanging from the ceiling in each room. No longer did the heavy acrid smell of coal oil lamps permeate the rooms.

Dora and her young daughter stayed alone in their isolated home while Jim worked the night shift in the coal mines. The loneliness, the creaking and settling of the newly built house, the cacophony of woodland creature sounds coming from the velvety dark woods terrified the young mother. She encouraged her younger sisters or brothers to visit often.

Chickens roamed about the yard. Running free were deer, wild turkeys, rabbits, squirrels, and other creatures in the dense woods surrounding the property.

Gail left the porch swing and walked over to a patch of daisies to pick some for her mother. She heard a sound behind her. It was the old rooster that didn't like her and ran at her when she got near him. She didn't like him and tried to shoo him away but he kept coming at her and she screamed.

"What is wrong with you?" asked her dad

"That old rooster is after me," screamed Gail as she ran for the porch swing.

"He won't hurt you," called her dad as he rounded the corner of the house.

"Yes he will."

One day when she was playing in the yard, the rooster tried to flog her and now she was terrified of him. She begged her mother to make him into a chicken dinner, but was told he'd be too tough to eat.

"Daddy, I ain't seen no big white bird come out of the sky holding a baby like Grandma said. Maybe that stork bird is already in the house and pecking on Mommy. That could be why she's hollering."

Jim smiled at Gail's comments but had no intention of explaining to his daughter how babies are made.

Gail ran to the screen door again trying to see what was happening inside and her Grandma shooed her away.

"Jim, keep this child away. She's got no business looking through this screen door."

"Come with me," said her daddy looking frazzled and nervous. "Let's go to the back yard and wait with the others.

Women were in the kitchen cooking a meal of country ham, cooked cabbage, sliced tomatoes, green onions, and corn bread for the noon meal to feed the family and neighbors who had gathered in to celebrate the baby about to be born. Existence was not easy and there was little excitement or amusement in the rural mountainous areas. A birth was a joyous occasion.

Just then someone called for Gail and her daddy to come inside. There were several women gathered around her grandma who was holding a little red baby.

Jim marveled at his beautiful, healthy son with all his fingers and toes, then anxiously went into the room where his wife was resting after her long ordeal.

Gail watched as her grandma lowered the little red baby down into a dishpan sitting on the kitchen table and gently scooped warm water onto it. Gail could see that the baby was tiny with a head of black hair.

"This is your baby brother," said Grandma glowing with pride.

The baby seemed to be enjoying the feel of the warm water on its skin. Gail reached up to touch its tiny red foot. She squeezed it and the little red baby began to cry.

"Stop that, Gail," her grandma scolded.

The baby stopped crying, but Gail thought it looked funny when it squinched up its face, closed its eyes, opened its mouth and squalled so she reached up and squeezed its foot a second time and sure enough it cried again.

Grandma smacked her hand and made her get away from the table. Gail ran to her mother who was resting with her eyes closed but she turned her head when she heard her daughter call.

"Did you see your little brother?"

Angel Wings

"Uh huh, but I didn't see no big stork bird."

Her mother smiled and said, "Your brother's name is Michael."

"No! No!" said her grandma from the doorway. "His name is Bobby Joe after his two grandpas, Bob and Joe."

Dora shook her head and said, "No! I want to name him Michael. That is the name I've picked out. His name will be Michael."

"His name is Bobby Joe. We've already written Bobby Joe on the birth certificate." Dora was too weak to argue and Jim didn't get involved. He defied his mother when it came to getting the doctor, but she won the battle of names.

Gail went back outside and climbed into the swing, her favorite place. Every now and then she would slip through the door into the front room to peek at the little red baby sleeping next to her mommy. She wanted to pinch the baby's tiny red foot to see it make the funny face, but she didn't want it to cry and wake up her mommy who was sleeping so peacefully and not hurting any more.

"I don't believe no big white stork bird brought my little brother. I think that doctor brought that baby in his black bag," Gail said out loud as she dropped one foot to the porch floor and pushed the swing back and forth . . . back and forth and contemplated the mystery of what happened in the front room of her house on this warm summer day, June 22, 1941.

Lantern in the Morning

A Day in the Life of a Mountain Schoolteacher in the 1920s

You can count the seeds in an apple, but you can't count all the apples in a seed. When you teach, you will never know how many lives you will influence. You are teaching for eternity. ----
Karen Jenson

The old clock on the mantle above the fireplace showed four-thirty. Joel snuggled deeply into the warm feather bed and gathered the quilts about his chin. Chills went up and down his spine as the wind shook the windows and whistled around the corners of the white wood farmhouse.

Joel sighed, threw back the covers and gingerly touched the icy floor with bare feet. He quickly lit the oil lamp and hurriedly dressed. With practiced ease, he soon had the carefully banked fire roaring in the fireplace and chasing the chill from the freezing bedroom.

In the kitchen, the old black cast iron cook stove swallowed the wood poked into the firebox and spit forth a few sparks and feeble flames, then burst into being. Last night's water had frozen in the rose patterned pitcher on the wash stand but water in the cook stove reservoir was soon warm enough for his morning ablutions.

Joel woke his wife, and then slipped bibbed overalls and a heavy coat over his neatly pressed suit, shirt and tie. Large, wet snowflakes were racing each other to the ground as the warmly bundled farmer stepped outside into the blustery December darkness. Joel lit the kerosene lantern that hung on a nail outside the kitchen door, and its yellow light helped him make his way down the snow-covered footpath toward the barn. The lantern swung back and forth while the wintry winds whipped the young man's coat against his legs.

Daylight was still hours away, and Joel braced himself for the farm chores that must be done in the cold darkness before leaving for the little mountain school. He taught a roomful of children from the surrounding mountain farms. Being both a farmer and a teacher left little time for anything but work.

Snorting, pawing horses, softly mooing cows and calves, and short grunts from the pig pen were familiar sounds to the young farmer. Hanging his lantern on a peg and working easily and rapidly, he soon had all the animals fed and the cows milked.

The barn cats purring around his legs wanted their share of the warm milk. Joel poured a generous portion in their food pan.

A foaming milk bucket in one hand and a lantern in the other, he crunched his way back to the house as the wind and snow stung his face.

"It feels good in here," he said to his wife as he entered the kitchen.

Welcome heat from the cook stove engulfed him. Removing his outer clothing, he washed up and sat down for a hearty breakfast of hot biscuits, cooked pork swimming in gruel, eggs, fresh country butter, strawberry jam, and a steaming cup of strong black coffee.

"The snow's already several inches deep. I didn't wake the children. It's too cold for them to go to school, and you ought not to go either," said his wife

"I'll go and if none of the pupils show up, I'll come on back. You stay in today, and I'll do the outside chores when I get back."

His wife, knowing there was little use in arguing, began to stuff biscuits with jam and pork for his lunch. She filled a jar with buttermilk, wrapped the biscuits and a fried apple pie in kitchen towels made from flour sacks and placed everything neatly in Joel's dinner bucket.

With the lantern lighting his way, he tucked his dinner bucket under one arm and his satchel under the other and trudged his way through the dark snowy woods. The only sounds were the crunch of his boots on the icy snow and the wind singing through the trees. The two-mile journey to the little mountain school seemed especially long this morning as Joel waded the snowy fields and woodlands.

The devastating depression of the 1930's was still several years away. In a few short years, the local bank would collapse under poor management and take down with it all of Joel and Virginia's hard earned savings, even the inheritance from her father. Those dark days were ahead. Today Joel's thoughts focused on the need for books.

Books were precious and difficult to find; the school had so few of them. Joel had heard about some books for sale in Kentucky. If this snow let up, he would ride his horse over the mountain on Saturday and try to buy some. The school had only a dozen or so books, and they were worn even though the children used thumb pads to save wear and tear on the pages.

Alone with his thoughts, he soon found himself at the river's edge. Since there was no bridge, the agile young man usually walked the rocks that jutted out of the shallow water; however, this morning the river was frozen. He tested the ice, found it safe and walked quickly across the narrow river.

Finally, the woods gave way to a clearing and he saw the dim outline of the little rough plank structure where he taught more than twenty children of all ages and abilities. When he reached the school house, he was cold but invigorated and refreshed.

Angel Wings

As he pushed open the unlocked door, the mingled odors of chalk, damp wood, past lunches, children's bodies, and musty well-worn books filled his nostrils -- the unmistakable smell of a schoolroom. He liked the familiar, comfortable feeling of being in this place where children learned.

On a table at the front of the room, Joel deposited his belongings and set the lantern down near the old wood-burning, pot-bellied stove. Getting the fire started and the room warm was a daily chore in winter. Competently, Joel used the wood from the wood box and soon the flames were licking the inside of the little potbelly stove. The fire felt good.

Joel noticed when the children moved too close to the little stove, the homespun material in the girls' long skirts and the boys' long pants steamed from the outside dampness. However, when they moved a few feet away, they felt cold. Most were not bothered by the cold and went about their lessons with few complaints.

Daylight was now coming through the two small windows on either side of the room. By the time the schoolmaster had made his preparations for the day, the morning was in full bloom. He stepped to the door to breathe in deeply of the clean, crisp, mountain air.

Joel noticed the snow had stopped and the wind had died. The calm and beauty of the snow-covered forest surrounded Joel as the quietness and serenity stirred in him a feeling of total oneness with nature. So totally caught up in the moment, he accidentally stepped off the porch and fell face first into a snowdrift. He picked himself up, brushed himself off and howled with laughter. Too bad his pupils were not here. They would love to see their teacher's dignity compromised.

Sounds of approaching children reached his ears. Most came on foot while a few of the lucky ones were brought on horseback by their parents. Joel didn't ride his horse because there were no provisions for horses at the school.

At nine o'clock, Joel stepped to the door and rang the small hand bell. He noticed that only ten pupils braved the weather. The children reluctantly left their snowball fighting. The bell was the signal to "take up books," meaning time for lessons to begin.

Rough plank benches with neither desks nor backs provided the only seating for the children; however, some of the more fastidious parents brought small chairs for their youngsters because of the prevalence of lice and a rash the mountain folks called itch.

Joel took the roll, had the pledge of allegiance to the flag, a reading from the Bible, prayer, and then the children began their schoolwork. The teacher worked diligently with them over the reading books until morning recess.

A bucket of water drawn fresh by Joel from a hand dug well in the schoolyard provided the only refreshment for the children. They shared a drink from the common dipper. When the need was there, they used one of the two small toilets at the edge of the woods. One for the boys and one for the girls and each fully equipped with a seat and a catalog. Recess over; it was back for the lessons.

"Get out your slates, pupils. It's time for arithmetic."

The screeching noise from the slates as the children worked problems sounded much like a roomful of excited chattering squirrels. Penmanship followed arithmetic class.

"Time for noon hour," Joel said as he took out his gold pocket watch and saw that it was twelve o'clock.

Most ate as quickly as possible so they could get outside to play. Some enjoyed corn bread and sweet milk mixed in tin buckets, others brought cold sweet potatoes, still others had a tin cup of pickle beans with molasses poured over them, and a few were munching on thick slabs of cornbread smeared with lard. Joel watched closely to see that everyone had something. His wife always put in an extra biscuit or two.

After the noon hour, Joel rang the little hand bell to signal the children to their afternoon lessons. The weather kept the young ones away. Had they been there, they would have worked on their penmanship and listened quietly as the older pupils had their lessons in geography, history and spelling. The children enjoyed spelling bees each Friday. Joel always had a prize for the winner, usually a coin.

After the school day ended, the children trudged through the snow to the multitude of chores waiting for them at home. The young teacher was alone again, surrounded by the quiet woods; the only sound the burning wood settling in the stove and an occasional gust of wind turning the corner of the school.

As Joel made preparations to leave, his day was far from over. There was the two-mile walk through the crusty snow with the wind stinging his face, the farm chores waiting to be done, papers to mark, wood and water to be carried in, and fires to bank.

The young father's favorite part of the day was the evening meal with his family. After the meal, they gathered around the fireplace and shared the events of the day. The family retired early, said their prayers and fell asleep in soft, warm feather beds.

His wife touched his shoulder, "Joel, its morning." The old clock on the mantle showed four-thirty and time for another day.

Meggy May

"I was led oftener through the Realm O Briar than the Meadow Mild."--- Emily Dickinson

"We need to talk, Meggy May," said Poppy walking into the kitchen where she was preparing supper. "Jess came by here today while you were at school. He asked if it'd be alright to come to see you."

"Why does Jess want to see me?"

"Maybe he wants to take you for a ride in that new car of his. I don't understand why his family spent good money for that machine when there ain't but a few rutty dirt roads to drive on."

"What did you tell him, Poppy?"

"Well, I told him he could come. He said he'd be over on Saturday."

She knew her poppy was pleased that Jess was interested in her. With eight kids to support and barely enough food to go around, she understood that Poppy wanted her to marry.

Meggy did think Jess was cute, but wild. She was a bit scared of him. He was an only child and was spoiled by doting parents. He stared at her in church and winked when she looked his way. The other day when she was washing clothes down in the creek

Angel Wings

below the road, Jess came puttering by in his Model A and blew the horn. He wanted her to go for a ride; she turned him down.

Saturday came and so did Jess. He took her in his car to a party at his friend's house. He tried to put his arm around her but Meggy would have none of that.

The weeks passed and Jess came visiting several more times.

"Meggy May, I talked to your poppy and told him I want to marry you. I think he wants us to marry."

No, thought Meggy. She did not want to get married. She was almost nineteen, and she had dreams. She wanted to study nursing when she graduated in the spring. Her parents did not have the means to send her, but she was determined to find a way.

The year was 1936 and the country was in hard times. Meggy's poppy lost his job at the logging company and couldn't find another one, but he did have a whiskey still up in the mountains. Money from the still, odd jobs here and there, vegetables from the garden, fruit from the trees in the meadow, and honey from the beehives kept the family from going hungry, but there was little money for anything else.

Her mother was sickly from chronic bronchitis and having nine babies, one died in infancy. Another baby came along before her body recovered from the one before. Meggy often wondered why her parents had so many children when they didn't really seem to enjoy any of them. Meggy was the oldest and for most of her childhood, her mommy had a little one clinging to her skirt, one in her arms and one in her belly. The older children helped raise the younger ones. The young woman remembered when she was twelve and carried her two-year old brother on her hip where ever she went during the whole summer.

"Meggy May," said her poppy one evening at supper, "marry that boy. His parents teach school and they've got that big farm. They live better than most of the folks in this mountain. He's a good match for you and you better not miss your chance. I'm tellin' you to marry him."

Meggy May

The young woman had never disobeyed her father so she told Jess she would marry him. Maybe Jess and his parents would help her realize her dream of becoming a nurse.

The only decent outfit she had was a black skirt and white blouse. The skirt was shiny; it had been pressed so much. She wore it to school but it was not appropriate wedding attire. Her aunt offered to make her a dress as a wedding present. The dress was green and it looked nice on Meggy's slender body. With her shiny black hair and blue eyes, the young woman did not realize what a beautiful bride she was. Jess did.

They married in his parent's back yard. She looked at this man who was now her husband and she realized she barely knew him and she really did not like him that much. There was no honeymoon. Jess told her they would be living with his family until they could build a house of their own.

"Jess, your parents don't seem to like me. They didn't want you to marry me, did they?" It hurt Meggy that Jess let his parents treat her the way they did. He didn't answer her; he walked away.

The wedding night was a disaster. Meggy, naïve and scared, had not been prepared for the marriage bed.

Her irate husband got up the next morning and said with disgust in his voice, "Get your things together. I'm taking you home." He left her on the road in front of her house and drove away in his car.

Meggy was glad to be home, but she knew her parents would not be glad to see her. Her heart was heavy as she trudged toward the house. She sat down on the porch to collect her thoughts. She would try to get them to understand how unhappy she was.

"Meggie May, what are you doing here? Where is Jess?" asked Poppy walking onto the porch.

"Jess ain't here. I want to come home. I don't want to be married. I don't like being married. Besides Jess's parents don't like me."

"How do you know this, Meggy May?" asked her poppy impatiently.

"Well, his mother told me they had someone else picked out for Jess and her family had money."

Days passed without a word from Jess, and Meggy worried that any day her poppy would send her back. Her mommy didn't say anything one way or the other.

Her heart dropped when she heard Jess's car stop on the road in front of the house. It was not Jess; it was his daddy and he wanted to speak to Poppy. They stood outside the house and talked for several minutes.

"Meggy May," called Poppy. "Come out here."

"Yes, Poppy," she dreaded what he would say.

"Jess's daddy has come to take you home. He says you're Jess's wife and people will talk if you don't come back. Jess's daddy don't like gossip. Go on with him, Meggy, it's your place."

Tears welled up in her eyes as she contemplated what she must do.

Meggy May did go back to her husband and bore him two children. They weathered the financial storms of the depression, the ration stamps of WWII, the mellow fifties and the unrest of the sixties. She and her in-laws were never close, but through the years they learned to tolerate each other. She had a strong faith in God that sustained her.

Several years after her husband's death, someone asked Meggy May to rate her thirty-eight years of marriage on a scale from one to ten with ten being the best.

"I would rate my marriage at a one," she said. "No, on second thought I would rate it a minus one."

Meggy May lived her life quietly. Her Bible was a comfort and a guide for her life. She never had the love she craved from her parents or her marriage, but her children loved her dearly. Her home was open to her family when one of them needed a place to stay or a good hot meal.

High school graduation never became a reality for Meggy May, nor did she realize her dream of becoming a nurse. She quit school a month before graduation because she did not have the money for graduation expenses. Neither her husband nor his family offered to give her the money she needed, even though they could easily have afforded it. She was so intimidated by them, she would not ask for help.

Meggy lived thirty-five years following the death of her husband. Her mind remained sharp and her faith strong, but advanced age and illness took its toll on this extraordinary lady. Surrounded by family and friends who loved and respected her, Meggie closed her eyes, reached out her hand to Jesus and stepped through the door into eternity.

Broth and Jello

Never a tear bedims the eye that time and patience will not dry. --- Bret Hart

Cream cheese on crackers and ginger ale, Kathleen's favorite bedtime snack, did nothing to quell the queasy feeling in her stomach. As a matter of fact, this queasy feeling was staying with her most of the time lately.

Day followed day and Kathleen's sick feeling continued. She could not shake it. She wouldn't let herself dwell too much on her fears that something was really wrong with her.

Maybe the change of life was on the way. After all, she was nearing forty years old. She convinced herself this was the problem.

As the sickness continued, irritability joined it. She dragged herself through each day as if walking through sand. She knew her family and co-workers could see the change.

At the end of the day, Kathleen was exhausted both mentally and physically. She prayed just to get through the days. She took herself to the doctor. He did a pregnancy test and it was negative, but he told her there was a problem. He wanted her to see a specialist, because he thought she might have a tumor. When you go for your appointment, be prepared to stay. The doctor may want to operate immediately

On the day of her appointment, Kathleen went with a heavy heart. She worried that she may have a serious health problem, and if she did, who would raise her two children. That possibility squeezed her chest so tight that she could hardly breathe.

After a careful examination by the specialist, the frightened young woman sat up dreading to hear what he might say. Scenario after scenario ran through her mind and none of them good.

"This tumor you think you have will come out in about eight months. You are pregnant. Sometimes pregnancy tests can be wrong. Yours was," quipped the doctor.

Shock registered on Kathleen's face. "Say that again."

"You are pregnant, but you don't have to have this baby, you know. Your age makes abortion a viable option," said the doctor. He began talking to her about the advantages of ending the pregnancy because of the possibilities of birth defects at her age.

Kathleen immediately came to her senses and realized the doctor had misunderstood her reaction. Abortion for her was not an option. Once a seed has been planted and you dig out the sprout, there is death to the plant. Same with conception, you dig out a growing life and there is death.

"I am only thirty-eight years old and I am not too old to have this baby. You misread my reaction of shock as negative. I'm relieved and happy I'm pregnant and I don't have a tumor. I want this baby, and even if I didn't, I wouldn't kill it," Kathleen answered shakily as the shock had not quite worn off.

The doctor wished her well and handed her a book entitled, *Your Pregnancy*. Her husband was waiting for her in the lobby. Kathleen went through the door and to the car. She got in and did not speak. She handed her husband the book and neither of them said a word until they reached the front door of their home.

Her husband spoke only one sentence, "Your mother will kill me." He knew Kathleen's mother did not want her daughter to have a third caesarean section. He dreaded her reaction. However, as the months went by, the family happily began to prepare for a new addition.

Kathleen awoke on New Year's Eve with a dull ache in her back. As the day wore on, she felt as if a belt were being tightened around her waist. A phone call to her doctor's answering service gave her no peace of mind. He was out of town for the holidays.

"Go to the hospital and someone will see you there," said the voice on the phone."

Night was falling as the family made their way to the hospital. Kathleen was frightened; the due date was still five weeks away. It was too soon.

At the hospital it was confirmed that the baby was coming; a nurse located a surgeon at a New Year's Eve party. The surgeon came, delivered a healthy baby girl and went on his way. The baby weighed six pounds, obviously a mistake in the due date. Her parents named her Elizabeth.

Later that night, a nurse brought Kathleen a tray with a bowl of broth and jello. The doctor ordered this for you. When he comes to see you tomorrow morning, he will order a regular diet.

Morning came and so did the broth and jello, but no doctor. This time the jello was green.

"I'm supposed to be on a regular diet starting this morning."

"Broth and jello is the order we have for you," said the person bringing the meal. "Check with the nurse."

"I will," Kathleen said and she did.

"We are trying to find the doctor who gave the order. Doctors are sometimes difficult to locate on a holiday week-end," said the nurse.

Lunch came and more broth and jello. This time the jello was orange. For dinner, she was brought more broth and jello. Each time the jello was a different color.

By Sunday morning, Kathleen was so hungry she cried to her husband to go to McDonalds for a hamburger and fries. Her husband was conflicted; maybe there was a reason for the diet.

Each meal on Sunday brought more broth and jello. The nurses were sympathetic but would not change the order. Arguing with them did no good. They kept telling her they were trying to reach the doctor, and were puzzled as to why he had not come in to check on her.

Her husband did sneak in a milk shake on Sunday night. Kathleen had never tasted anything so good.

On Monday morning, the doctor who delivered the baby came in and apologized to Kathleen.

"I forgot to change your food order. As a matter of fact, I forgot about you. I'm pleased you are doing so well and there were no complications."

"You forgot me! That does explain why you didn't come to check on me. Did you know I had broth and jello for seven meals?" Kathleen said with indignation.

The doctor grinned and said, "I'm sorry. You'll be happy to know that you have a regular breakfast coming this morning. You and the baby are doing fine, so I'm releasing you to go home tomorrow."

On the way home the next day, Kathleen told her husband about the doctor's confession.

"At least he was honest, and I forgave him. However, I don't believe I'll be able to look at broth or jello for a long, long time."

Kathleen left her job and became a stay at home mom. The family began spending more time together. They sat down for meals which was something they didn't often do before the baby arrived. Elizabeth's presence pulled them together in happy ways. She was God's gift to them.

There is no feeling better than a baby's soft, fuzzy head nuzzled against your neck and cheek, thought Kathleen.

After she was all grown up, Elizabeth would jokingly say, "I looked down from heaven and saw this family with two healthy kids and enjoying their new home. The parents were getting older but working in jobs they enjoyed and active in church and communities activities. Everything was going so well for them, I asked God to let me join them so I could shake things up a bit. God has a sense of humor so he honored my request."

Gladys

Some people no matter how old they get never lose their beauty—they merely move it from their faces into their hearts. --- Martin Buxbaum

"I'm gonna put a sign in the yard that says No Vacancy," Everett said with a tease in his voice that barely covered what he really felt. I think he was tired of the steady stream of company that came to his door, but was too kind to show it.

Living in sunny Florida made Gladys and Everett a magnet for family and friends. The young wife's loving nature and gracious hospitality made anyone who came to her door feel welcome. We were no exception. Gladys was my husband's sister and we all loved her dearly. We called her Glad. The name fit her because of her sunny disposition and positive attitude.

Helping Glad clean the dishes after supper one night while we were visiting her family yet again, I ventured into the living room to check on my son.

Our two kids loved Glad and Everett's little dog, Toby. He was a cute little poodle and would sing along with the radio or television. When a song began to play, Toby would stick his nose in the air and howl along with the music. This was in the 1960s long before YouTube was created. Today that dog would be a sensation.

"That is the smartest dog, and he is so cute," I said as I picked up my five year-old son's glass of lemonade from the floor where he was playing with Toby. I decided to drink the remaining lemonade in the glass before taking it to the kitchen for washing.

"Why are you laughing, Everett?" I asked holding the lemonade glass in my hand.

Everett continued to laugh so hard the tears were sliding down his cheeks.

"What is so funny?"

"You shared that lemonade with the dog. He lapped from the glass just before you came into the room."

"Why didn't you tell me? Why did you sit there and watch me drink from a glass the dog drank out of?"

"I wanted to see your face when I told you."

Everett had a mischievous streak that came out sometimes. He was a tease and if he could 'get you', he loved it. I liked Toby but I certainly did not want to drink after him.

One of my first remembrances of Gladys occurred when I began dating her brother. He took me to visit his sister on my sixteenth birthday. She baked a cake for me. I thought it was the most beautiful cake I had ever seen. It was decorated perfectly. My mother always baked a cake for my birthday but it was never decorated. I took the cake home and didn't want to cut it because it was so pretty. My brother had other ideas! I relented and the cake was soon gobbled up by my family. It tasted as good as it looked.

Gladys, the oldest of six children, was a determined child according to her mother. She tells the story about a time when her daughter was twelve years old. The children got new shoes each year when the school year began. Gladys picked out a pair of high heels that she wanted. Her parents told her that she was not old enough for high heels and anyway such shoes were not appropriate for school wear.

Gladys

Several days later her mother sent her to the store for some needed items and told her to charge them. Gladys did as she was told; however, she also bought the high heels she wanted and charged them. The happy young girl wore the shoes home so her parents could not take them back.

Having the high heels was worth the punishment she knew she would get when she arrived home. Things did not go as she planned. Her dad sawed the heels off the shoes and made her wear them. That was her punishment. She laughs about the experience now, but says at the time, it was not funny because the shoes pinched her feet.

Gladys married Everett at seventeen. In the years to come she gave birth to two babies. The first one died at three months of diarrhea and the second baby lived only a few hours. The heartbreak the couple suffered was immeasurable. In her mid-twenties God blessed Gladys and her husband with a beautiful son. They named him Ronnie and they took great pleasure in watching him grow. He was sunshine in their lives. With all the love and attention they gave this golden child, his spirit remained sweet and unspoiled.

This young mother liked challenges, and taught her son not be afraid to try new things. Ronnie though he and his mom could do anything. Rarely did the two shy away from something they were interested in accomplishing.

Gladys graduated from beauty school and worked as a beautician for a while. The talented young woman excelled in cooking, crafts, and even carpentry. One day when we were visiting, I noticed the doorway into the kitchen was changed from one corner of the living room to the other.

"You have changed the entrance to your kitchen since I was here," I remarked.

"I decided the doorway would be more convenient on this side of the room so I moved it. My son helped me," said Gladys. Her son was seven years old at the time.

"You two did that by yourselves? You tore the wall down and rebuilt it with the doorway in the other corner. It looks like a professional job. You are amazing," I said with admiration in my voice. "You make beautiful quilts and crafts; you are a great cook, you can sew and crochet and now I find you are a carpenter, too. Is there anything you can't do?"

The talented young woman was not one to boast. She seemed unaware of her amazing talents and accepted them in a matter of fact way.

When their son turned thirteen the family moved from Virginia to Florida. There her husband started a business repairing cars and selling gasoline. They were young, energetic and not afraid of hard work. They earned the success they achieved.

The young wife studied bookkeeping in Florida and worked for a time at a newspaper. She also kept books for her husband's business. Life moved along seamlessly for many years. The mother and father took great joy in watching their son grow and excel in school, sports and in time his job. His marriage to a beautiful young woman brought two beloved grandsons. More blessings came later with four great grandchildren.

Fate reared its ugly head and cancer took her husband. A torturing grief devastated Gladys but her inner strength and faith sustained her. Several years later the unimaginable happened. Cancer took her beloved son, her only child, the light of her life. Her grief was inconsolable with pain so deep it bruised her soul. This pain and loss lives with her, yet she finds the courage to face each day. It helps that her grandsons and great grandchildren love and dote on their granny. Her soul is warmed by the sunshine of their love.

Gladys is now ninety-three years old and in poor health, yet she has a sweet spirit and so much love to give. Flowing back to her is love and respect from her extended family which is quite large.

One of these days, this sweet little lady will be whisked off to heaven to meet the beautiful family she has up there. We hope that won't be for a long, long time. A light will be gone from this world when God takes Gladys home.

Jilli

Angels are always near to those who are grieving, to whisper to them that their loved ones are safe in the hand of God. --- Eileen Elias Freeman

For a small southern town, the affluent neighborhood where eleven-year old Jillian lives boasts a number of people from varied cultures.

Jillian, her family and friends call her Jilli, became friends with a Muslim girl who lives on her street. They enjoy playing together and sometimes talk about their views of God and heaven. These chats often confuse Jilli and lead to many challenging questions for her family.

"Mommy, how do we know that we are right in our beliefs and other people are wrong about God and heaven?"

Jilli's parents, committed Christians, fielded her questions as best they could. They wanted her to know that it was okay to question and they would seek answers from God's word.

Petite for an eleven-year old, blonde haired Jilli has beautiful eyes that shine with intelligence. She and her younger sister Josie are home schooled and both excel in their studies. Testing shows them to be above their grade level. Their three-year old brother,

Hudson, when displeased with his sisters has an excellent throwing arm for whatever object happens to be at hand.

Thanksgiving dinner was a fun time for the family until a phone call from her paternal grandmother summoned the family to the hospital. The grandfather recovering from a heart attack had taken a turn for the worse. Sadly, before the family reached the hospital, her grandfather had made the transition to heaven.

The family was devastated with grief. Jilli in her grief had many questions about her grandfather. She wanted to know about heaven ... what it looked like, what people did there, was her grandfather happy in his new home, was he with Jesus ... was God real?

One day when Jilli was in her room with the door closed, she decided to pray. Kneeling down on her knees, she prayed that God would show her a sign if He was real. She turned her head and there in her room stood an angel.. She opened her door and called for her mother. Rushing into the room, her mother found her little daughter jumping up and down with excitement.

"Mommy, there's an angel in my room. I prayed for a sign that God was real and He sent an angel."

"Where? I don't see it."

"You don't see the angel? There are the wings and they sparkle! I can't see the face clearly because it is shadowed, but the angel is here! I'm standing right beside it!" said Jilli pointing with awe at the magnificent vision before her and frustrated that her mother could not see it.

"Jilli, I can't see it, but I believe you do. God heard your prayer, and He answered."

The angel stayed for a short time and at one point seemed to be kneeling in prayer. Gradually the vision disappeared.

While her mother didn't see the vision, she knew something extraordinary had happened to her daughter. The angelic vision in answer to a little girl's prayer brought comfort to a grieving family.

Melissa

"Trust in the Lord with all your heart and lean not on your own understanding."
Proverbs 3:5 [KJV]

Melissa is a remarkable woman. Her life is a testimony to the power and mystery of God and how He can restore health and vitality to a body and mind abused by alcohol and drugs. Melissa is a role model for people who give up because life kicks them in the teeth.

Until Melissa turned four, life was normal for her family. With her father in the air force, they lived in many different parts of the country. Life took a chaotic turn when Melissa's father walked out on the family leaving them stranded in New York City. With limited job skills, broke, and having no support system, Melissa's mother was forced to move the family back home to the mountains to live with relatives.

The grandparents built in their back yard a small three-roomed house with no indoor plumbing. Melissa's mom moved them into the little house and found a job as a waitress to support them.

The grandmother agreed to keep the children while her daughter worked. She constantly reminded them that they were a burden and a bother. Often, the children were sent outside to relieve themselves because their grandma didn't want them to mess up her bathroom. She told them they peed too much.

If the grandmother or the aunt baked goodies, the children were not allowed to have them. The goodies were kept for the men's dinner buckets. The grandfather and uncle worked in the coal mines.

When Melissa was old enough to attend school, she went happily. She loved school and stayed near the top of her class through her elementary years.

Seventh grade proved difficult for Melissa. Seventh graders were divided into several groups with the most academically successful in the first group and ranging on down to the least academically successful in the bottom group. Melissa was selected to be in the top group but felt uncomfortable and wished she were in a lower group.

The students in the highest group were always talking about going here and doing this or that with their families. Melissa's family never went anywhere. Her mom didn't drive, and there was no money for extras. She had little in common with her class, so she found friends in the lower academic groups where she felt accepted.

Melissa let her grades slide. If they had groups in high school, she did not want to be put in with the elite group again. She wanted to be with her friends. The only divisions in high school, though, were the ones in the heads of the students. The social cliques kept Melissa isolated to the fringes.

School was a pain and things weren't going well for Melissa at home either. Her mother's boyfriend didn't like Melissa so he shunned her. He took her sister to school, but would not take Melissa. With no other transportation, the young girl was forced to walk to school. She felt she had no one on whom she could rely or trust.

Melissa

Melissa says she remembers praying that God would never let her bring children into the world to be raised like she had been.

It seems as though everyone failed Melissa – her family, her school, even the church where she sometimes attended. She and her family went to church when someone offered them a ride and that was not often.

"I became a wild child at thirteen and just gave up on people. I began to use alcohol and drugs," but she emphasized, "I never put anything up my nose or in my veins."

At 16, Melissa married an immature mama's boy whose main focus was drugs. She immediately realized instead of getting a home and someone to love and care about her, she simply sank deeper into the mire of uncertainty and poverty.

Too often, Melissa's husband stayed home doing drugs with his buddies while his young wife went to work at a fast food restaurant. During this time, her school attendance was sporadic. Melissa was scared most of the time and didn't know what to do, or where to turn. The marriage lasted six weeks.

With her marriage ended and with no place to go, she reached out to the only person she thought might take her in – her grandma. To her grandma's credit, she did give Melissa a place to stay; however, the desperate young girl's lifestyle didn't change. With her grandma's help, and even though she was high on drugs much of the time, she did manage to graduate from high school.

Confused and unsure about her future, Melissa decided to marry a man she didn't love but who was a good friend to her.

"He was a nice guy, and he loved me. I thought I could grow to love him, but it didn't happen. I couldn't make the marriage work with someone I didn't love, so we divorced," she said with sadness in her voice.

Sometime later, Melissa met Len. He was twenty-eight and Melissa was eighteen. Soon after they met, Len left to go to Louisiana. He called Melissa and asked her to come to him. He told her he couldn't live without her.

Melissa went but soon realized she had made a big mistake. Len tried to kill her several times. He wanted to pimp her, and he wanted her to dance in sleazy places. Melissa refused. Len beat her, humiliated her, held a gun to her head and isolated her in a house far away from civilization. She was not allowed to contact anyone.

With the help of a chance female visitor to the house who understood what was going on, Melissa was able to get away.

"Len followed us and shot at the car. The girl's car was an old trap, but we managed to reach a restaurant and get inside. The manager was a big man and Len was a wimp. Len only wanted to hit women; he wouldn't tangle with men. Intimidated by the manager, he left and I never saw him again," said Melissa.

The young girl moved to Florida where she met Ray. She liked him right away so they moved in together. Melissa says they lived a pretty rough life style with a bunch of characters that loved to party as much as they did.

Melissa chuckled as she said, "I could drink most men under the table."

One Sunday, Melissa and Ray were headed home to Florida following several days of partying in North Carolina. Melissa began to have odd sensations in her body. She stressed that she had not drunk any alcohol nor used any drugs that day so she didn't believe that was the cause.

Melissa said, "I kept seeing all these bumper stickers and billboards with religious messages. They were jumping out at me and the sensations in my body were making me feel quite ill. When I asked Ray if he saw the messages, he acted as if he didn't know what I was talking about.

"I could feel my legs getting numb and there were pains in my chest and running down my arm. I could barely breathe. Ray stopped the car and laid me out on the shoulder of the highway. I could feel my whole body getting numb.

"There was a strange hand on my cheek very gently turning my head toward the traffic-filled highway and a voice saying, Can those people save you?

Melissa

"Up above my head there were swirls of dark smoke. I felt my spirit leaving my body and heading upward toward the smoke. It was the most horrible, terrifying feeling I have ever had. I can't find words to describe my terror. I felt I was in the middle of a battle being waged between the soft voice with the gentle hand on my face and the ghastly swirls of smoke above my head. I believed I was dying so I screamed to Ray to please accept Jesus as his Savior and go to God so he wouldn't go to the horrible place I was going.

"Ray was leaning over me and looking at me as if I was crazy. My body was completely numb except for one shoulder and my head. I knew the devil was rejoicing because he thought he had me. The gentle voice kept speaking to me that only He could save me but the choice was mine.

"I did make the choice to obey that gentle voice which I felt was coming from Jesus Christ. The feeling immediately started to come back into my body. Ray had no idea what was happening. He thought I was dying, and took me to the nearest emergency room.

"The doctor could find nothing wrong with me but emphasized that the symptoms sounded like a heart attack. I didn't tell the doctor about the spiritual experience. Just thinking about that day sends cold chills down my spine. God fought for my soul and the devil lost. Thank God, I made the right decision."

After this experience, Melissa was very confused. She didn't understand what had happened to her. She had given up on church when she was thirteen, and until now had wanted no part of religion.

"I want to talk to a preacher and learn how to become a Christian," she told Ray

Ray couldn't understand the complete turnabout in Melissa. Confusion was eating away at her and Ray was at a loss in how to help her.

Melissa found a church near her home and went in search of the preacher. She had very little knowledge about different religious beliefs and how some churches can be rather narrow in their views.

"Keep in mind," Melissa said, "my lifestyle dictated my dress. I wore short shorts and skimpy tops with straps and no bra. This was the way I dressed; my clothes fit the way I lived.

"When I walked into the church, some women were there. They stared at me disapprovingly but I went on in and asked for the preacher. I was so desperate to talk to a preacher that I didn't react to the behavior of the women toward me.

"The preacher took one look at me, glanced at the women, and then hesitantly asked me to come into his office. His eyes seemed wide with fright as he looked at me. He jumped behind his desk as if for protection.

"I told him about my life, about what had happened to me on the shoulder of the highway, and that I believed Jesus had saved me. I stressed to him how desperately I needed help in understanding how to become a Christian."

"You will have to go back and remarry your first husband," said the pastor emphatically. "If you want to become a Christian, that is what you must do. That is the way it has to be."

Melissa was shocked at his words and tried to explain, "I don't love my first husband. I don't even know where he is. I haven't seen him in years. I love Ray, the man I am with now."

The pastor stressed to her that it didn't matter. If she wanted to become a Christian, she must do as he told her. Melissa left the church more confused than ever. She went outside to find Ray lying on top of the car listening to his music. He looked at Melissa and asked if she felt better. She didn't!

Melissa's life was broken and she was earnestly seeking God's direction for her life. The minister seemed uncomfortable with her and focused only on her marital situation instead of telling her of God's love, encouraging her to pray, emphasizing to her that the Bible is God's word to her, and sharing with her some Biblical truths. Whatever the reason, his cold judgmental attitude left Melissa more broken than ever.

Melissa

Ray had hoped the preacher would be able to iron out Melissa's confusion, but she seemed more troubled than ever. He hurt for her and did not know how to help. Ray was not a Christian and did not know how things worked but it seemed to him that after hearing Melissa's experience, and seeing her desperate need to understand what had happened to her, the minister would at least try to interpret the experience using scriptures from the Bible. Wasn't that what preachers did?

Melissa thought seeing a counselor might help her, so she found one in the yellow pages and called for an appointment. When Melissa arrived at the office, the counselor seemed to be in a hurry. The counselor asked about her problem; Melissa shared her confusion and her desperate need for help.

"Honey, you were raised in them mountains where people are narrow-minded and uneducated. You just go out and have a good time and party like you always done. Forget about this religious stuff," said the counselor as she cleaned off her desk in preparation to leave.

Melissa, an intelligent young woman, recognized incompetence when she met it. When she came outside, Ray asked her if she felt better, but he could tell she didn't.

"Maybe the counselor, even with her poor grammar, has a point. Maybe I just need to forget about everything," said the troubled young woman

Ray agreed and that night they went to a bar.

"It was ladies night," Melissa said, "which is nothing more than the opportunity for women to get drunk so guys could pick them up. I was a heavy drinker so I got several long island teas and downed them all. By the time we got home at three a.m., we were both wasted."

The next morning, the hung over young woman was not happy with herself. She knew she had made a bad decision the night before. She did not want to live like this anymore.

She picked up her Bible. For some unknown reason, she had always carried the family Bible with her wherever she moved. She never read it, just kept it with her. When she picked it up, the Bible opened not to the Scriptures but the question and answer section at the back.

Some of the questions mirrored her situation and the answers seemed to be speaking to her. Melissa decided to go back home to the mountains. She felt she couldn't live with Ray anymore since they were unmarried. She couldn't explain it; she just knew she had to return to her roots.

Ray bought her a bus ticket. He didn't beg her to stay. He knew she was being torn apart by the confusion inside of her and desperate to find someone to help her make sense of what had happened on the shoulder of the highway. Both thought it might help her to get away from the friends and other temptations in Florida.

When Melissa returned to her hometown in the mountains of Virginia, she had no money and no place to go. Her aunt let her come and stay in her home. She had no clothes. She left all her clothes in Florida because they were inappropriate in her new life.

Melissa's aunt went to a second-hand store and bought some dresses, but they didn't fit. Melissa didn't care; she wore them anyway. The hurting young woman ate hardly anything, and her weight plummeted. Her clothes hung on her gaunt frame.

"Something was happening to my mind," Melissa said. "Sometimes I felt like climbing the walls, and shattering into a million pieces."

As Melissa's body began cleansing itself from the powerful grip of drug addiction, she suffered immensely. She chose not to take any medication to help with the physical, emotional and mental pain. She chose instead to pray and read her Bible.

"When the church doors were open," Melissa said, "I was there. My attitude toward church was changed. In my younger days, I wanted nothing to do with church but now I could not get enough. It didn't matter what church or what denomination, I just wanted to be in God's house with God's people and have them pray for me."

Melissa

One night during prayer meeting, she began to sweat and tremble, so she left and found a dark corner in one of the empty rooms to hide. She rolled into a fetal position and cried tears from deep inside her soul.

"When everyone left," Melissa said, "I began to scream and literally tried to climb the walls. The preacher came to me but didn't know how to help. He sat with me and prayed until I calmed down

"Many of the people in the churches probably thought I was insane," Melissa continued, "but they kept praying for me and I continued to heal. God didn't make it easy for me, but He never left me. I felt His love and support, and this is what got me through the darkest times.

"Gradually my mind cleared without the aid of any recreation or prescription drugs. With the prayer and support of God's people and God's love for me, I began to get control of my life."

Ray called Melissa and told her he had been reading his Bible and had accepted Christ as his Savior. He wanted to come to where she was living. Ray had no money and no place to stay. Melissa wouldn't live with him, and she didn't want to get married until she felt she was ready.

With nowhere else to go, Ray slept in a lawn chair on her aunt's porch during that cold mountain winter. He did eventually find a job, got a place to live, and he and Melissa were married.

As Melissa and Ray grew in their Christian walk, their future looked bright and they wanted to start a family.

Melissa said, "We visited a fertility specialist and tried for five years to conceive, but God didn't see fit to grant this desire. I know now that He had other plans for Ray and me."

The couple decided that since they couldn't have biological children, they would take foster kids into their home. The first two children were little boys, ages six and four, who had been abused. Eventually, they were able to adopt both children.

This was the beginning of a God-centered life caring for thirty foster children, sixteen of whom they adopted.

"All the children we have taken into our home have been hard-to-place children who have special needs," Melissa said, "and they each have a story. We eventually made the decision to only take in those children who were eligible for adoption."

After several years Melissa and Ray were blessed with two beautiful biological children. That brought their number to eighteen. The couple faced many trying times through the years, but they radiate peace and happiness. Melissa and Ray have a special glow about them. They are an amazing couple. Their happiness seems to shine out of their souls. Their faith is tremendous, and they believe God will make great things happen for their children.

The years have passed and only seven of the children remain at home. The others have gone in search of their own destiny, and all are doing well. Some are serving their country in the armed forces, some are in college and others have married and established families of their own.

Melissa recently received her master's degree in counseling. She is working full-time with special-needs children. God is still using her in mighty ways.

"God gave me another chance at life," Melissa said, "and gave me a wonderful man with whom to share it."

Melissa and Ray live a life of Christian service and many special children have been the winners.

Ruben

*"I have fought a good fight,
I have finished my course,
I have kept the faith."
II Timothy 4:7[KJV]*

Ruben sauntered into the college counseling office to talk about his schedule. With each visit, the talk moved from his class schedule to other things going on in his life.

As the young student talked, he would duck his head then look up with those big, blue, soulful eyes to see the reaction to his comments. He was an intelligent, sweet-spirited young man with a vulnerability about him that touched the counselor's heart.

The divorce of his parents lay heavy upon Ruben. He didn't like what was happening at home yet he was powerless to stop it. Ruben loved both his parents but was especially close to his mother. Being a very compassionate young man, he was devastated by the divorce.

Ruben didn't want to stay with either parent, so he left and bunked in with one friend and then another. Bouncing around from house to house and trying to stay in school was not working for him so he dropped out of college.

Without training in something he wanted to do, Ruben had no choice but to take whatever job he could find. The job he found was with a local company that fielded customer complaints.

After Ruben left school to enter the work force, the counselor lost touch for several years. On hearing that Ruben was ill, she was concerned. She contacted Pearl, Ruben's sister, a former student at the college. The two of them talked several times about her brother's life.

Pearl cared deeply about her brother and was disappointed when he dropped out of college. Pearl's goal was to become a pharmacist. She worked diligently, stayed focused and reached her goal. She wanted Ruben to have a career goal, too, and seek appropriate training. Yet, no matter how much his family wanted the best for him, they could not get inside his head and make his decisions.

"One night at the end of my first year of pharmacy school," Pearl told the counselor, "Ruben jumped on the bumper of a truck, fell off and was run over; the driver didn't see him. His leg was pushed past his chest and over his shoulder breaking his pelvis in three places. Skin was torn from his back exposing his kidney."

Ruben cheated death but for several years his life was filled with pain so great he took prescription drugs or anything else that would give him some relief from the excruciating pain. Ruben had experimented with drugs before his accident, but no drugs of any kind had ever taken control of his life until after the accident.

The horrific accident set in motion a chain of events fueled by pain and bad choices. Some of the decisions he made during this time led to actions resulting in a burden of guilt he carried with him. He felt God wouldn't want him because of things he had done. His sister assured him that God loved him and would forgive him. All he had to do was ask.

Ruben was visiting his sister when she saw a black oozing place on his rib and she asked him, "What is that on your side?"

Ruben shrugged his shoulders, "I don't know. It's been there for a while."

"I think we need to have that looked at by a doctor." Pearl remarked with concern showing on her face.

Thus began the nightmare for Ruben and his family.

Pearl went with her brother to the first visit with a doctor and the removal of the spot on his rib. After a week, Ruben returned to the doctor's office to have the stiches removed and get the mind numbing results... malignant melanoma. The fear rampaged like a wild thing through his heart and mind as he and his family confronted the cold, dark realizations that death might be near.

Ruben was twenty-six years old, his father's son, his mother's baby, his sister's best friend and his brother's hero. He was also about to begin the biggest fight of his young life with an opponent that didn't play fair.

Joby, Ruben's brother, was serving his country in Iraq. Ruben did not want him to hear about the cancer until he finished his tour of duty and came home. He felt his brother was already in harm's way and worrying about him would be a dangerous distraction. The young man didn't want anyone outside his immediate family to know about the cancer.

Ruben was referred to the University of Virginia at Charlottesville. An MRI was clear, but three of five lymph nodes on his left side were black and questionable. The doctors weren't sure whether the black color was from cancer or the tattoo on Ruben's chest so they decided to remove all five lymph nodes. The doctors didn't believe that radiation therapy or chemotherapy was necessary but suggested he take interferon treatments.

After the doctors told him that suicidal ideation was one of the most prominent side effects of interferon, Ruben elected not to have the treatments. He agreed to have himself evaluated every three months for the first five years. He was told that if there were no signs within five years his recovery rate would be eighty-seven percent.

"We all came home with hope in our hearts. My brother felt he had a second chance, and he was determined to make some positive changes in his life," Pearl said with tears in her eyes.

Changing a life style is a difficult process and doesn't happen overnight. The young cancer survivor was living in the black squeezing grip of prescription drug dependency. With help from his family, he was determined that drugs would not be his master. He wanted to get his life back on track. Strength of character was something Ruben had in abundance; he only needed to sweep some debris away to find it.

Facing his own mortality helped Ruben see his life clearly for the first time in a long while. He had made some bad decisions that led to abuse of his body and mind, but that time was behind him.

"One day Ruben came to me at work and asked for my help. He was heartbroken and crying," said Pearl. "He said he was so tired of the life he had and the people with whom he had surrounded himself."

"I offered to send him to a rehab program but he refused. He said he could do it on his own; he just needed to know we were there for him."

Ruben's first decision was to move away from his present circle of friends to lessen the temptations. He asked the girl he loved to come with him, but she refused. This brought him emotional pain, but he was focused and determined to make a clean break from his former life.

The determined young man moved fifty miles away to East Tennessee State University, rented an apartment and enrolled in the university.

Trusting people was difficult for Ruben. He kept them at arm's length. He did have one confidant—his mother. He told her everything, but she couldn't reach inside and straighten all the pieces of his heart and soul. He would have to do this for himself. With the support of his family and sheer force of will, Ruben did clean up his drug dependency problem.

Ruben dealt with a lot of loss in his young life. Losing the security of his home, losing his health for several years after being run over by a truck, losing control of a prescription drug problem, losing the girl he loved, and now in danger of losing his life to a potentially fatal type of cancer.

Down inside Ruben seethed a cauldron of emotions that found some release through his writings and his art. This outlet for his emotions was healing, and would later prove to be a comfort for the family.

With the support and love of his family, the young man was finally getting control of his life. The family was elated that he was doing well physically and academically. He was studying to be a message therapist. Having had so much pain himself, he wanted to bring comfort to others.

Life was going well for Ruben and his family. Joby came back safely from Iraq after his second tour of duty, and a baby was on the way for his sister, Pearl. His three-month x-rays had all been negative. Each time the doctors had given him a clean bill of health. The positive things happening in the family were a welcome change from the worry and pain of the past few years.

Pearl said, "Christmas, 2004, was a happy time for our family."

In January, 2005, Ruben was looking tired and stressed. He came by the pharmacy in February and told his sister that every time he ate, he felt sick and he had pain. He questioned his sister about liver pain and what it felt like. Pearl was concerned about him but since all of his cancer tests had come back negative, she thought he might be having some problems with his gall bladder. Ruben often worried about the condition of his liver because of his years of drug use. He thought he might have weakened it.

In March, Ruben called his mom and asked her to come and get him. He said he felt too sick to drive. She went to him and brought him home. A few days later after seeing the doctor, they were called to the office for a consultation. The doctor dropped a bombshell when he said the cancer had spread to his liver, lungs, spleen and pancreas with hot spots on his bones.

Pearl said, "As the doctor talked, Ruben never once looked at him. He kept his eyes on Mom. Ruben felt her reaction would tell him whether he could fight the cancer or if it were hopeless. Mom bit the insides of her mouth to keep from breaking down because she knew the effect her reaction would have on Ruben."

Pearl continued, "Ruben was admitted to the hospital and began to deteriorate rapidly. He was always a neat and tidy person, but it had become more and more difficult and finally impossible for him to shave. He got weaker and weaker with the cancer taking everything from him. He couldn't sit up because there was so much fluid.

"After my baby was born, Ruben tried to sit up and hold the baby, but he couldn't. Finally he became so weak and so filled with fluid he could barely breathe.

"When I sat the baby on the bed with Ruben, the two looked into each other's eyes. There seemed to be an understanding between them that was unexplainable. My baby had recently been born into the world, and Ruben was getting ready to leave it. Maybe there was a connection between them that is a mystery to the rest of us," said Pearl.

Death was now a constant companion for Ruben. Pearl says she told him not to be afraid and he said he wasn't. He had always told them that he would die young; he would be the first in the family to go.

Ruben's dad was with him one night when the sick young man asked who else was in the room.

"There is no one else here but the two of us," his dad assured him.

"Someone else is near my bed," Ruben told his father.

His father says he then felt the presence himself so strongly that he stepped out into the hall to compose himself.

God may have sent an angel to prepare Ruben for the journey that he would soon be making. We know he made his peace with God from this line in one of his poems, "I smile and laugh now, my soul at ease."

This uplifting message from the poem was a gift this sweet-spirited young man left for his grieving family.

The day before Ruben left for heaven, his doctor was in his room and he said to Ruben, "You're hanging in there. God must be holding your hand."

The young patient had not been able to respond to anyone for two days but he said quite clearly to the doctor, "Not God, it is Jesus."

The next morning, his mother asked him, "Ruben, who were you talking to last night? You mumbled all night."

Using what little strength he had left he said, "Not talking, praying."

Ruben died that night.

God took Ruben and left his family with a hurt that chafes the soul, yet, they can take comfort in the words from one of his poems, "I shall see you soon, if you should ever need me, look to your heart."

A line in another of Ruben's poems says, "Far away and free, free to be me."

Ruben traded his disease-ridden body for a new one and left this shallow world for heaven. He is now free to be himself without ever again worrying about what doctors find wrong with his body or what people think of him.

Some live longer lives and have time to smooth out the rough spots as they grow and learn; others have lives that are cut much too short. Ruben's life was too short but life handed down a decision for the young man over which he had no control He could have become bitter but instead he developed such a sweet spirit that he was an inspiration to all whose lives he touched.

Ruben thought of others to the very end of his life. He was an organ donor. Someone is seeing today because of him. He wanted his body donated to a teaching hospital. Medical students would have the opportunity to study a cancer-ridden body and gain knowledge to help treat people suffering from the disease.

Death was not the end for Ruben, only a transition to a different kind of life. This amazing young man moved through death to the gates of heaven. With his new spiritual body, a twinkle in his eyes and a smile that could light up a room, he met Jesus who welcomed him home.

Scotty

A Dog Story

"You think dogs will not be in heaven?" I tell you, they will be there long before any of us". --- Robert Louis Stevenson

"We want this one!" Mark and Lisa ran to her father and me with the newspaper showing a cute little dog, "Pet of the Week."

"You promised." they said. "This is the one we want."

When we reached the shelter, we learned that the puppy shown in the paper had already been adopted. The worker told us there was another puppy, a Scottish terrier, ready for adoption and we could have him. When the puppy came out to greet us, the first thing he did was puddle on the floor.

"Oh, he does that when he's excited," said the worker.

He was a beautiful puppy with black curly hair, a large head, and square shoulders. He had the look of a Scottish terrier, but he was just a loveable mutt. Mark thought that was just fine. "If we were dogs," he said, "we'd be mutts, too."

The dog adopted us immediately; the children named him Scotty. The shelter worker was right; excitement went straight to Scotty's bladder. The newspapers we brought with us saved the carpet in the car from getting soaked.

My husband was principal of the local high school. We lived just across the highway from the school. Our house and yard and the school property became Scotty's territory. He followed Harold to work each day and lay on a mat outside the school's front door. He greeted the students, teachers, and anyone else who entered or exited his building. At night, he guarded his turf and if a human or an animal came around, he barked to let them know they were encroaching on his territory.

Scotty could be quite annoying. While most of the students and teachers tolerated him and some even grew fond of him, he tried the patience of the teacher who was in charge of pictures for the annual. Most of the group pictures were taken outside and Scotty felt he should be a part of anything involving his students. The teacher did her best to keep Scotty out of the pictures but he outdid her. She finally gave up and let Scotty have his way. Scotty can be seen in many of the outside group pictures in the school annuals standing proudly with his students.

Another of Scotty's endearing traits was his friendship with cats. Pittypat, the family cat, and Scotty became friends. Pittypat loved to lie on Scotty's back and sleep. Pittypat was a loner; she did not like people. But for some reason, she loved Scotty. Visitors were amazed at the bond between the dog and cat. Scotty would even allow Pittypat to eat from his food bowl. At night they curled up together and kept each other warm.

Scotty's acceptance of cats extended to a little kitten someone left by the road in front of our home. The kitten ran in front of a car and was badly hurt. Scotty pulled the kitten to the side of the highway and curled himself around the kitten to protect it until we came home. When we found them, it was too late for the kitten.

Scotty

Living so close to school property was not pleasant. There were some students who loved to aggravate the principal. They threw tomatoes at our house and even on occasion rocks through the windows. We no longer felt comfortable living so close to the school so we moved to an area some distance away.

Scotty found it difficult adjusting to a new neighborhood. He missed his students and the pats on the head and attention he received at school.

He began visiting the neighbors, because he loved being around people. Some of the neighbors tolerated him; others wanted him gone from their property. He loved lying in the neighbors' cool, soft flower beds to their dismay. He especially enjoyed visiting the neighbors when they had cookouts. Several times to our embarrassment and the neighbors' anger, Scotty stole hamburger patties or a steak from a neighbor's grill. The phone would ring and one of the children would go get Scotty, bring him home, and put him in the garage until the cookout was over.

We tried chaining him in the yard with a long leash, but his neck and shoulders were so strong, he'd pull the stake out of the ground. If he couldn't get the stake up, he would whine and bark until the noise disturbed the whole neighborhood. For some peace and quiet, we would let him loose.

Scotty was a sweet-natured dog. He loved everybody, and he thought everybody felt the same about him; of course, this was not the case. He though anybody who came in the neighborhood was a friend.

One of the most terrifying experiences of my life happened one quiet, peaceful night and still sends chills down my spine.

My six-week-old daughter was sleeping soundly upstairs in her crib. Lisa, Mark and their father were attending a basketball game at the high school. I was looking forward to relaxing and reading for a while when I heard a sound much like firecrackers hitting against the house. Shortly after the popping sound, I heard Scotty whimpering from the patio.

When I opened the sliding glass doors, I screamed. Blood was everywhere. Scotty had been shot and had shaken himself. It looked as if someone had sprayed red paint on the glass doors and the patio. Scotty was standing in a pool of blood. I realized with horror that the sounds I heard were not firecrackers but gunshots.

I ran to the phone to call my husband. Luckily, he was in his office rather than in the gym. I told him to get home quickly and leave the children at the game; they would be safer there. When I went to care for Scotty, he was gone. I called for him again and again but he did not come. I could not leave the baby to search for him. I feared the gunshots had killed him. The children would be devastated; we all loved Scotty.

In minutes, my husband was home. He called the police, checked around the house to make sure the shooter was gone and searched for Scotty to no avail. With the police on the way he returned to the school to get the children.

I was terrified that someone would shoot my family before they could get back home. I turned off all the lights in the house except the one in the downstairs den. I went upstairs to be near the baby and wait for the police.

My husband was barely out of sight when I heard the sound of screeching tires. Trembling, I ran to an upstairs window. There in front of our house was a young man leaning out the passenger window of a car and pointing a rifle at the only lighted window in the house, the den window. He shot several times hitting our car and the house but missing the window. The shooter and his buddies pealed out and were gone before the police had time to arrive.

The police came and my family returned safely from the school. Mark and his father went in search of Scotty but could not find him. His father convinced Mark to come inside and promised the two of them would search for Scotty come morning. I wanted them safely in the house and so did the police. I was terrified the shooter would come back and try to kill us. I believed that anyone who would shoot into an occupied house meant harm to those inside.

The police stayed outside our house all through the night in the event the shooter came back. He didn't.

The shooter, caught later in the week, was a student at the high school. Police found marijuana and alcohol in his car. The police learned the drug fueled teen was angry and went on a shooting rampage because he had been disciplined at school for a rule infraction. He and his buddies had fried their brains with drugs. Their idea of fun was to shoot an innocent dog that had never done anything but love them, and to shoot up our home and the home of the assistant principal. The angry young man could have killed innocent people.

We believe Scotty recognized the students in the car and ran to greet them, and they shot him. The next morning, our son was out looking for Scotty before anyone else was out of bed. Mark combed the area and did not find Scotty. He was broken hearted, as were we all.

Several days later, my husband was mowing the lawn, when one of the policemen came by to ask how we were doing and if we'd found the dog. My husband sat down in the driveway to rest while he talked to the officer. He felt something lick the back of his neck.

"Is that your missing dog?" asked the officer.

My husband turned around and there was Scotty. His fur was matted with blood and mud. Harold jumped up and called for the kids to come outside.

The officer rejoiced with us; we had Scotty back. The children grabbed him mud and all and rushed with him to the vet. The veterinarian told us that Scotty had many shotgun pellets under his skin, but that he would recover. The doctor removed as many of the pellets as he could, especially those about Scotty's face. After a warm soapy bath, and lots of loving care, Scotty was soon back to normal and visiting the neighbors.

Angel Wings

The phone calls from neighbors annoyed with Scotty became more frequent and one phone call especially frightened us for his safety. A neighbor called us and said she overheard someone talking about poisoning Scotty. She would not divulge the name.

We decided to take Scotty to my mother's farm. Mark and Lisa were disappointed but understood why we had to give him away in order to save his life. At their grandmother's farm, Scotty had the fields in which to run, and cows and horses to chase.

Scotty adjusted beautifully to his new life, and we could see him whenever we wanted. He'd give us a welcome lick, then go chase chickens.

I would like to say that life went back to normal, but something was taken from us that night that we never got back as a family. Never again did we leave the house with the trust that we once had. Rarely did my children or my husband leave the house that I didn't think about that terrifying night and only relax when I heard them come through the door.

The shooter was sent to a mental hospital rather than to jail. The policeman who interviewed him warned us to be cautious because of threats the mentally unstable teen made against our family and the family of the assistant principal. We learned from the officer the teen hated people in positions of authority; he abused drugs and was intellectually slow. The shooter stayed only a short time in the mental institution. With his release back into the community, both families lived with vigilance and uneasiness.

The shooter left me with more than a wounded dog, damaged house and car; he left me a changed person and a changed parent. I became overprotective and fearful for the lives of my family.

Only through prayer and the passing of time have I been able to forgive the hate filled, drug addled, and mentally unbalanced young man. I understand he is now in prison. It is my prayer that he will get the help he needs to turn his life around.

Teensy

One sweetly solemn thought
Comes to me o'er and o'er;
I'm nearer home today
Than I ever have been before
---Phoebe Cary

"Mary Ann, will you come over this morning?" Teensy spoke softly into the telephone to her step-daughter.

"Do you just want company or are you not feeling well? You sound rather melancholy this morning," said Mary Ann with concern in her voice.

"I'll explain why I need you when you get here," Teensy answered and hung up the phone.

Mary Ann wondered about the unusual tone in her stepmother's voice. She put her thoughts aside as she showered and dressed; she would find out soon enough.

Now that Teensy knew Mary Ann was coming, the determined woman put the rest of her plan into action. She neatened the house, bathed, and put on her prettiest pink nightgown and robe. This was to be a special morning.

Angel Wings

The little gray-haired lady sat down by the window to enjoy the sunshine and wait for Mary Ann, her late husband's oldest child. The two of them had grown close through the years. Teensy never had children, but she loved her husband's four children as if they were her own.

Her beloved Timothy was in heaven now making the angels laugh, and she missed him terribly. Her frail little body relaxed against the chair as she let her mind travel back in time to the 1940s. Their love story was a sweet memory tickling her thoughts this morning.

Her real name was Ruth, but Timothy called her Teensy from the first time they met in the hospital sunroom. Teensy was tiny and frail, and to Timothy she looked like a little pink flower sitting there in her wheelchair. He rolled his wheelchair over to her and said, "Hi, Teensy." From that day Ruth had a new name. Even the hospital staff started calling her Teensy.

She accepted the nickname and she and Timothy became friends. Meeting in the sunroom gave them the opportunity to chat and support each other in their recovery from heart problems.

This new friend fascinated the delicate young woman. As sick as he had been, Timothy never lost his positive attitude and easy sense of humor. He brought smiles to the hospital staff and anyone else that happened to be around him.

As the days passed, the frail young woman enjoyed the kind-hearted man's company more and more. So what if he was several years older, she thought he was cute, and he made her laugh.

Timothy was skinny, with a few hairs keeping each other company on his head. He seemed oblivious to his faded pajamas, well-worn robe and scuffed house shoes. He appeared to be completely comfortable with himself.

Teensy had beautiful gowns and robes and most of them were pink—pink gowns, pink robes, pink slippers and a pink lap robe. Timothy said to her, "You must really like pink. The only thing not pink is your pretty brown hair."

Teensy

The nurses were behind the coincidental meetings in the sunroom. They thought the older man with his sense of humor would be good for the frail woman's recovery. He was! His compliments and fun-loving nature raised her spirits.

Teensy was getting more and more interested in Timothy, but he saw her as a fellow patient and friend. Because she was so much younger, he would not let himself think of her in any romantic way. He knew the time would come when they would be released and now it was here. He dreaded telling his little friend goodbye.

The nurse rolled his wheelchair into the sunroom and there was Teensy all pink and smiling. He looked at her and realized how much he was going to miss not seeing her. They had come from opposite ends of the state to this hospital. Traveling across the state to visit would not be easy for either of them. The two of them exchanged pleasantries and Timothy knew it was time to say goodbye.

"I'm being released at the end of the week, Teensy. I want you to know that I'll really miss you."

Teensy felt her throat tighten. She did not want to live away from this man. The weeks they had spent recuperating together were some of the happiest of her life. She had never had a boyfriend; her weak heart had kept her confined to a restricted life.

"Timothy, I'm being released, too. Please take me with you, and let's get married." Teensy pleaded with tears in her eyes.

"Have you lost your mind, young lady? I'm twenty-five years older than you. Your family has money. I don't. Your family would never allow you to marry a poor man with four grown children. I don't think my children would be any too happy either."

Teensy finally convinced her beloved companion that marriage would work for them. On the day they were to be released, the hospital chaplain married them in the chapel where they often prayed together. The bride-to-be dressed in her prettiest pink gown and robe and the prospective groom dressed in a new robe and pajamas (a gift from the hospital staff) pledged their love to one another.

Mary Ann came to pick up her father and was stunned with the news that a wedding had taken place shortly before she arrived. No one on either side of the family was aware of the marriage. Teensy had yet to break the news to her family. She knew they would be shocked because she had not told them of her friendship with Timothy.

The newly wedded groom took his bride home to the mountains and introduced her to a surprised family. Timothy's wife had died many years before with cancer, and their father marrying again at his age was something they did not expect. They were especially concerned how, with his compromised health, he could take care of this tiny frail wife.

There was a knock on the door and the sound brought Teensy back to the present. She never tired of bringing back the sweet memories of her life with Timothy. She never regretted leaving a life of financial comfort for a life of genteel poverty. She loved her husband and she knew he loved her. They had few material things during their twenty-seven years of marriage, but they were happy together.

Timothy's children grew to love their step-mother and fully accepted her into the family. Teensy was thankful for their love and kindness. Her own family never accepted the marriage, and she was estranged from them for the rest of her life. This loss hurt her, but she never regretted marrying the man she loved.

Their strong faith in God sustained them through the years. Their faith enabled them to deal with the behavior of Teensy's family and the illnesses they both faced through the years of their life together.

The doorbell rang so Teensy put her memories aside, got up to answer the door and welcomed Mary Ann.

"Mary Ann. I'm glad you're here."

"What's going on? You sounded mysterious over the phone."

"Well, I'll come right to the point. I'm going to go to sleep this morning and when I wake up, I'll be with my beloved. I want you here with me; I don't want to die alone. Now, come with me to my bedroom."

"Teensy, what are you saying? Are you ill? You are joking with me. Right?" questioned Mary Ann as she followed her step-mother to the bedroom.

"No, I am not joking. It is my time, and I'm going to Timothy. An angel came to me in a dream last night. He told me that today I'll be changing this worn out, sick body for a spiritual one. I believed him!

Mary Ann replied emphatically, "Teensy, you are not going to die this morning. It was only a dream."

Teensy appeared not to listen to what Mary Ann was saying. The woman stood speechless as her step-mother removed her pink robe, pulled back the covers and slid into bed. With her head on the pillow, she smiled at her step-daughter, took a deep breath, closed her eyes and lay very still. In a minute or so she opened her eyes and seemed to be surprised. She took another deep breath, closed her eyes and lay still. When her eyes popped open, she seemed to be not only surprised but disappointed. The persistent woman continued the process several more times and seemed to be getting more annoyed each time she opened her eyes.

Mary Ann pulled a chair up to the bedside, held her step-mother's small wrinkled hand and decided to humor this dear little woman until she came to her senses. Another deep breath, and the room became deathly quiet. Mary Ann jumped from her chair and realized her step-mother was no longer breathing but had a sweet smile on her face.

Can a person believe so strongly that they can even will their own death? This is a question Mary Ann's family still ponders years after the death of their beloved step-mother.

The Sweater

"Wouldn't it be wonderful if, as you read these words, an angel whispers in your ear, speaking of God's unconditional love for you, words you can hear if you listen carefully?" ---Mitch Finley

The little old lady's eyes glowed when she spied the cardigan sweater hanging on the department store rack. She gently lifted the cardigan from the hanger and held it to her chest. The sweater's butterscotch color triggered a memory from long ago, causing tears to glisten on her weathered cheeks.

She remembered how she and her friends loved to window shop walking home from school. Poodle skirts, saddle shoes, and cardigans adorned the department store windows in tantalizing display in the fifties.

"Oh, look at that cardigan sweater. It's the color of butterscotch pudding, and there's a poodle skirt to match" said Emily with longing in her voice.

"And that poodle skirt is the color of caramel icing," said one of her friends mocking her.

"All this talk about pudding and icing is making me hungry. I'm going home. See you all tomorrow," said another friend.

The girls said their good-byes and went their separate ways. Emily took one more look at the outfit then headed home. Cardigans and poodle skirts were all the rage at school and Emily had neither. The popular girls at school with their ponytails and attitudes wore outfits like the one in the window. She wanted to be like them but her reflection in the store window showed a skinny fourteen-year old girl with wispy, stringy brown hair.

Emily's imagination was a place she often lived, and she went there often, much to the dismay of her parents and teachers. Now, lost in her daydreams, she could see herself walking down the hall at school in that cardigan and skirt. She sighed and walked on knowing money was tight for her family since building their new home. Maybe her mom could squeeze out the money for just the sweater. She'd forego the skirt if she could have the sweater.

"Mother, I saw the most beautiful cardigan in the window of Berry's today. Please, can I have it? It is so pretty, and all the girls have them," she said excitedly as she came through the door from school.

"I'm sure all the girls don't have them, but we'll discuss the sweater later. Do your homework, then your chores," replied her mother as she busied herself with preparation for the evening meal.

That being the only commitment Emily could get, she sighed and hoped for the best. The radio was blaring with Pattie Page singing "How Much is That Doggie in the Window." Emily didn't want that doggie in the window; she wanted that sweater in the window. She didn't have many clothes, but that butterscotch cardigan would be just the thing to spice up her meager wardrobe.

Emily's homework and chores done and supper over, her mother still had not discussed the sweater. Emily tried to bring up the subject but her mother only said they would discuss it later.

The next day was rainy and cold as Emily trudged home from school. Passing Berry's, she and her friends noticed the outfit was no longer in the window. Her friends assured her that none of them had purchased the sweater and skirt. Sadly, Emily made her

The Sweater

way home, called hello to her mother and made her way up the stairs

Emily loved her room with its rosebud wall paper and patchwork quilt. It was her haven. She could read, do homework, put her poems and stories on paper, listen to the radio or daydream to her heart's content. Many of her daydreams centered on the new history teacher. He was her secret crush.

When she opened her bedroom door, Emily's heart skipped a beat.

"Mother, I love you! Thank you! Thank you!" she said as she ran from her room to hug her mother.

On her bed lay not only the cardigan and poodle skirt, but also a new green winter coat.

"I hope you like the coat. It's getting cold, and I know your old coat doesn't fit anymore," said her mother enjoying Emily's reaction to her new clothes.

"Oh, Mom, they're beautiful," exclaimed Emily excitedly as she ran to try on her treasures. She preened and posed before the mirror and later could barely sleep in her excitement.

Emily bounced into the kitchen the next morning in her new clothes and asked her mother to braid her hair. She wanted her stringy hair braided and tied with white ribbons to match her white blouse.

"You look nice this morning, Emily," said her mother as she began to work with Emily's hair.

Emily hugged her mother and left for school feeling snug in her new green coat. Her cardigan felt warm and soft, and the poodle skirt bounced over her crinolines as she sashayed down the street. She could hardly wait to get to school and show off her new clothes to her friends.

As she walked happily along the sidewalk, a car pulled up to the curb and her heart began to do flip-flops. Calling her name from his car window was the object of her crush . . . the new history teacher. "Want a ride to school?" he asked.

"No, uh. . . er. . .thank you," Emily stammered.

No, thank you. Was that all she could say? She wanted to go but was much too shy to take him up on his offer. The dreamy new history teacher with his flippy hair and blue eyes had actually noticed her.

Her pleasure was dampened somewhat to see Chloe entering the school with no coat to cover her slight body on this cold winter morning. Emily, in all her new clothes, felt pangs of guilt as she followed Chloe down the hall. Rumor had it that Chloe had actually slept outside when her father didn't come home from his carousing. He evidently didn't care enough to make sure Chloe had a key to the house. Her mother had died of pneumonia when Chloe was small.

Although Emily didn't have a lot, Chloe had even less. On impulse Emily took off her new coat and called to Chloe.

"Chloe, I want you to have this coat."

"I don't want your coat." Chloe hated it when the other kids felt sorry for her. She did like Emily, though, because Emily didn't seem to look down on her because she was poor. Emily had even given her lunch money a few times and occasionally pencils and paper.

"This coat doesn't really fit me," Emily lied. "Here, just try it on."

Emily handed the coat to Chloe already regretting her impulsive decision to give the coat away. However, the feeling Emily got in her chest from giving the coat was warm and she did still have her new cardigan and skirt.

Chloe reached for the coat and pulled it against her slight body. Emily looked away, though, when she saw the raw emotion play across Chloe's face.

"Are you sure you want to give me this beautiful coat," asked Chloe.

"Oh, sure," said Emily. She did regret her hasty decision, but did not have the heart to take back the coat. Emily had a problem with acting first and thinking later.

Emily turned and walked down the hall with less confidence, and wondered what her mother would say when she found out

The Sweater

about the coat. She hoped her mother would get her another one when she heard about Emily's generous gesture.

Going to the school library was one of Emily's favorite times at school. She loved to browse the shelves for interesting books to read. It was warm in the library and Emily took off her cardigan and put it on the back of her chair. She lost herself in pursuit of a new adventure as she searched for a good book.

When she returned to her seat, she was horrified to see no sweater on the back of her chair. She sat down to calm herself but the tears were coming. She didn't want anyone to see her cry so she asked to go to the bathroom. She got control of her feelings and returned to the library to try to find the sweater but to no avail. Her beautiful sweater was gone.

The day started out to be a so great, but had gone painfully wrong. Unbelievably wrong! "This can't be happening! My beautiful coat and now my sweater are both gone," moaned Emily.

Walking home with the wind and cold whipping around her, she was freezing in her short-sleeved blouse. This morning she wore joy and self-confidence, but this afternoon she wore sadness and disappointment. She dreaded her mother's reaction when she learned what had happened. Emily left for school with a new coat, sweater, and skirt. All she had left was the skirt.

Her mother sat happily at her pedal sewing machine when Emily came into the house.

"Emily, why the sad face?" asked her mother.

Out spilled the whole sad story.

Her mother lowered her head onto the sewing machine and began to cry. This reaction was not at all what Emily had expected. Her mother didn't yell, or berate her for her careless behavior as Emily had expected. She just sat there and cried. Emily had rarely seen her mother cry and those tears were punishment too painful to bear.

"Mother, why are you crying?" asked Emily.

Building this house has put us on a tight budget. Your father and I sacrificed to buy those nice things for you, and there is no money to replace them. It was admirable of you to want to help that young girl, but this time you are going to live with your decision. You can wear my coat. Please, Emily, you must learn to think before you act. Someday, your impulsive nature could get you in real trouble," sighed her mother wearily.

Not that old black gabardine coat, thought Emily. She was really beginning to regret her impulsive behavior.

The next morning dawned cold and snowy. Emily pulled on her mom's old black coat and rolled up the sleeves. The coat was old but it was warm. Needless to say, she felt quite different on her way to school this day.

One of the smart-mouthed boys in the hall laughed and said, "Hey, Emily, is that your mother's coat?" Tears stung her eyes. She was hoping people would not notice the coat. It didn't help when later in the day she saw Chloe wearing the new green coat.

It's not fair Emily thought as she moped down the hall to her class. She did a nice thing by giving away her coat to a needy girl and then some mean person stole her sweater. Things like that were not supposed to happen!

"May I help you?" Asked the clerk

Emily blinked and pulled herself back to the present.

"Yes, please, I want to buy this memory . . . . I mean this sweater."

The clerk watched the little old lady as she walked slowly toward the door clutching the bag with the butterscotch-colored cardigan and wondered why tears glistened on her wrinkled cheeks.

Leaving the store another memory brought a smile to Emily's face. The next year when winter came, her mother bought her a beautiful new red coat.

Emily's mother asked her, "What are you going to do with this coat?"

"Keep it," Emily said emphatically, and she did!

The Letter Jacket

Too often we underestimate the power of touch, smile, a kind word, an honest compliment or the smallest act of caring, all of which have the potential to turn a life around. --- Leo Buscaglia

Carrying a bulging brown paper bag, the immaculately dressed man walked to the podium and set a mysterious brown paper bag on the floor. His lean frame, neatly combed blond hair, and easy bearing spoke of confidence and success.

Larry looked over the people at the banquet table and his eyes came to rest on the man being honored at this special dinner. Being a deeply feeling and compassionate person, he had difficulty holding his emotions at bay. Respect for one another was obvious as Larry began to talk about this man, Harold Lester, who had been his coach, his mentor and a father figure.

Harold's career spanned many years, first as a coach, then as an assistant principal, principal and in the latter years as an administrator in the central office of the school system where he spent his career.

As Harold listened to the speaker, he let his mind traveled back through the years to Larry as a young boy from a family of ten children whose uneducated parents were not prepared to take care of themselves let alone ten children.

Larry's mother had grown up in a family of fifteen and had known only poverty and struggle all her life. She married an irresponsible man who made no commitment to his wife or the precious children he helped to create. As a result, life was bleak for the family. Larry seldom saw his father, because his father was a rare visitor to the home.

Harold brought himself back to the present as he heard Larry saying, "Sometimes we had something to eat for supper and sometimes we didn't. Although Mother usually had a bite of something to give us for breakfast, it was never much. We lived in a three-room house with no indoor plumbing. The only water we had was what we carried from a neighbor's well. We didn't raise a garden so we subsisted on government surplus food."

Larry spoke about liking school because Coach Lester got him a job in the cafeteria, allowing him to have a hot meal and extra food every day for free. After physical education each day, there was the opportunity for a hot shower. Larry stressed how much the daily meal and shower meant to him.

As he listened Harold felt admiration for this man who earned his college degree and his success through hard work, sacrifice, and a positive attitude. He also respected the way Larry cared for his mother in her later years.

Larry told of a day many years ago when he was in high school. "I heard my name called over the intercom to come to the office. My heart jumped to my throat and fear began to creep up my body like a living thing. My knees were shaking as I slid out of my seat and made my way to the principal's office. I had never been in any trouble and never been called to the office. What had I done? I hadn't broken any rules, at least I didn't think I had."

Harold remembered that day when the sixteen-year old hesitantly stepped through the door. His unkempt blond hair and well-worn clothing belied Larry's potential. He liked the boy and saw that potential. He had been impressed with the intelligence in the blue eyes now wide with fear. When the young student was given a job in the cafeteria, he proved to be an excellent worker. On the football field he gave his best, as he did in the classroom.

Larry continued, "Coach Lester was the assistant principal and the football coach. Since I was one of his football players, maybe he wanted to talk to me about football; however, he also took care of most of the discipline. Fear grabbed hold of me again, especially with Coach Lester's paddle prominently displayed on his desk."

"Larry, there is a jacket here that someone ordered and didn't pick up. Try it on and see if it fits."

"I was relieved he only wanted me to buy a jacket, not punish me for some broken rule. I tried on the jacket and it fit, but I told him I couldn't buy it. He told me to take it on back to class with me.

"Walking down the hall in my new jacket, I dropped my head and felt my eyes get misty. I stroked and examined the new jacket. There was my name inside. How could that be? Someone else had ordered it, the coach said. How could my name be inside?"

Harold remembered that he had dismissed the lad quickly because he, too, had misty eyes seeing the look of disbelief mixed with awe on the boy's face.

Larry reached under the table and pulled out the mysterious paper bag. In that bag was the football letter jacket he had kept down through the years. He removed his suit coat and pulled on the treasured jacket. After all these years, it still fit.

It was obvious to the people at the dinner that the letter jacket was still a treasured garment. He told the group how he finally figured out that Coach Lester bought the jacket. Larry told how much that act of kindness meant to him.

Larry went on to tell how he was called into that same office again and given a class ring the coach told him was an extra one but had his initials inside.

Angel Wings

In closing, Larry reminded everyone how teachers, coaches and others who work with children are significant adults in the lives of those children. He told how these people have the power to change a life with a well-placed word or a kindness that a vulnerable child will soak up like water on a desert. Equally, these same significant adults using negative words and actions can have a devastating effect on vulnerable children.

Before he left the podium, Larry thanked Coach Lester for the kindnesses he had shown him and the positive effect those kindnesses had on his life. He stressed how many other lives this compassionate man had touched through the years.

As he watched the speaker take his seat, the school administrator was moved to learn that he had played even a small positive part in the life of one of his all-time favorite students.

Although he gave up his coaching position to become a high school principal, the former coach had a special place in his heart for the young men he coached. He called them "his boys" and followed their lives through the years. He rejoiced when he learned of their successes and grieved for them when he learned of their disappointments and sorrows.

He was especially proud of Larry who, from a young boy, faced life as a challenge and dared to rise above the limitations in his environment.

Messengers

"Are they not all ministering spirits sent forth to minister to them who shall be heirs of salvation." Hebrews 1:14

Samuel, agitated toward his wife, turned his face toward the wall and refused to continue their conversation. She didn't believe him when he told her about the late night visitors to his hospital room.

"I sat by your bed all night and only nurses were in your room," explained his wife with weariness in her voice. "We thought you were dying and now you are getting better. Let's not argue but be thankful our prayers were answered. "

Samuel wanted his wife to understand there would be no miraculous improvement had it not been for the three men who came to his hospital room and gave him the vial of medicine.

Over the last several months, Samuels's illness had taken its toll on both he and his family. His doctor treated him for ulcers, but the treatment had not worked. Samuel's fever, nausea and pain continued. Unable to find the cause of his problem, the doctor sent him to a surgeon.

The nightmare began in the surgeon's office when Samuel learned an x-ray showed a large shadow on his liver. The surgeon thought the shadow was a malignant tumor that may have metastasized. The only way to know was risky exploratory surgery. Samuel was willing to take the risk. The day of the surgery was a tense day for both Samuel and the family. Following the operation, the doctor came to the family with surprising news.

"We misdiagnosed Samuel's problem," explained the surgeon. "There is nothing wrong with his liver. The shadow we saw was an enlarged gall bladder. In fact, his gall bladder was so enlarged and badly infected that it came apart in our hands. This explains the nausea, fever, and pain. We are concerned about infection. His prognosis is not good."

Samuel could tell from the faces of the medical staff and his family that nobody expected him to leave the hospital alive. He hated all the tubes connected to him, especially the one down his throat.

He could see his wife beside his bed dozing in her chair. She looked exhausted. The rest of the family had long since gone home with the promise that she would call if there was a change in his condition. He dreaded the night ahead and what it might bring.

Samuel closed his eyes and the sleeping medication from his IV took effect. Sometime in the night, three men came into his hospital room. They were well-dressed in suits and ties and calmly began to talk to him. They showed him a small vial of medicine and told him the medicine would heal him but it was expensive. He must pay them one hundred dollars. They told Samuel that if he chose to accept the medicine, it came with conditions. His life would change.

Samuel paid the one hundred dollars and drank the medicine.

Daylight streamed through the windows and Samuel opened his eyes. He felt good. He couldn't wait to tell his wife about the visitors, but anxious man could not talk with the tube down his throat.

Sarah leapt to his bed when she noticed his agitation. She ran for the nurse who took Samuel's vital signs and found them normal. She called for the doctor. Soon there was much activity going on around Samuel's bed.

The doctor told the nurse to remove the tube from Samuel's throat and gave other instructions before turning to Sarah. There's been a dramatic change in your husband's condition. Last night he was gravely ill. I must admit it's most unusual for someone in his condition to improve so dramatically overnight."

"I can explain the change. Three visitors came to my room in the night," spoke the patient hoarse from the tube. Words began spilling out as Samuel told his story. The doctor and nurses listened with skepticism showing on their faces.

The doctor was quiet for a moment, and then he said, "Samuel, I don't have a medical explanation for this positive turnaround in your condition. It does appear something miraculous has happened to you. That was an interesting dream you experienced." With those words the doctor left the room assuring Samuel he would be back later.

Sarah felt her knees go weak with relief. She thought her husband was dying and instead he was getting well.

"I'm hungry," said Samuel as he raised himself up and rang for a nurse.

Sarah thanked God for answered prayers as she walked down the hall to telephone the children and tell them the miraculous change in their father's condition.

When Sarah returned, Samuel was sitting up in bed drinking a soda and eager to talk more with his wife about his three night visitors.

"That was a wonderful dream, Samuel, but there were no visitors to your room last night. I sat by your bed all night and no one came in but the nurse to take your vital signs."

"Sarah, three men did come to my room last night, they did give me a vial of medicine. I paid them for it, I drank it and now I'm getting better". His wife could see that Samuel was frustrated with her reaction.

"Samuel, you had a tube down your throat. You could not have swallowed anything. Furthermore, where would you get a hundred dollars?" said his wife trying to lighten the mood.

"Sarah, I did not think I would leave this hospital alive and neither did anyone else. That vial of medicine healed me. If it was only a dream, then why am I better this morning? Three well-dressed men did come to my room and they did give me medicine," argued her agitated husband.

Something miraculous had happened to Samuel as he slept, and Sarah was thankful. Just what it was she didn't know. She did not want to upset her husband again by questioning his "dream." She sat quietly and listened as he talked.

"I wonder what they meant by conditions and that my life would change?" Samuel said with wonder in his voice. He was not a religious man so he did not put spiritual connotations on his experience. When the family arrived, they were elated at the improvement in their father's condition.

After a few days the happy patient returned home. He related his story again and again to family and friends. They listened politely but most were skeptical. However, they did notice that Samuel was like a different person.

Robert, Samuel's father-in-law, was not in the least skeptical about the night visitors to his son-in-law's hospital room. Robert was a Christian and Samuel was not. Therefore, his father-in-law wanted to choose his words carefully. He wanted to use his son-in-law's experience to lead him to Christ.

"I believe you had an angelic visitation. God sent messengers to you, but it was neither the medicine nor the men that healed you; it was God. The vial of medicine was symbolic. By accepting it, you agreed to certain conditions. Your spirit met those men in your hospital room. I believe the conditions they were talking about involved a personal relationship with God.

"What am I supposed to do, Robert?"

"I think you must start growing spiritually by reading your Bible, praying, and attending church to fellowship with other believers." Robert prayed for God's guidance as he continued to witness to his son-in-law.

"When you make the decision to accept Jesus Christ as your personal Savior, and the Holy Spirit takes up residence in your life, a change will take place in you, Samuel. You will serve a living God who loves you so much that he sent his son to die on the cross for you. The decision you make will determine where you will spend eternity."

Samuel did begin to read his Bible, pray, and attend church on a regular basis. He did receive Jesus Christ as his personal Savior. He felt a freedom and peace he could not describe. He was thankful God gave him a chance to change his life.

Sarah believes her husband did have a supernatural visitation that resulted in a physical and spiritual healing. There was a dramatic change in every phase of his life. He truly was a changed man.

Samuel sought ways to glorify God with his life. He donated land and helped build a small community church. He took every opportunity to witness to others by giving his testimony. His greatest joy for the rest of his life was his relationship with Jesus Christ.

Mountain Path

For I the Lord thy God will hold thy right hand, saying unto thee, Fear not; I will help thee. Isaiah 41:13 [KJV]

The treacherous bends struck terror in the heart of Isobel, a home health therapist, as she steered her car down the dangerous one-lane unpaved mountain road. It was more like a path than a road. Looking on the right side the view showed a steep dropoff. There was no guard rail, and the road seemed no wider than the car. Once the she started down the mountain, there was no turning back. She had to keep going even though terrified she might slip in the gravels and end up at the bottom of the mountain. Another frightening thought . . . What if she met another car? There was no way she could back up.

Forty minutes later Isobel arrived at the isolated cabin of the home health patient. She had prayed as she slowly inched her way down the narrow path. Arriving at the cabin, the young woman felt herself tremble with fear at the thought of the drive back up that treacherous mountain road.

While she evaluating the patient, the therapist had a difficult time concentrating. She prayed for God to calm her fear. For her job in home health, Isobel had traveled to some isolated places with narrow mountain roads, but never anything like the one to this place.

"How do you get in and out on that road," she asked her patient."

"The few people who come here either walk or ride a small jeep. Didn't anyone tell you about the difficulty of getting in and out of here in a regular vehicle?"

"No one told me. I don't know if I can get my car back up that road."

The patient seemed concerned and cautioned her to be careful.

When the evaluation was over, the apprehensive young woman said her good byes to the patient. Making her way to the car, she prayed that God would give her a safe trip.

The feeling of impending doom was strong and she was trembling with fear as she started the car. She lowered her head closed her eyes and began to pray that God would surround her car with his angels.

Isobel insists from that point she remembers nothing until she opened her eyes and found herself back in town. How she got to where she was, she cannot say. She does not remember driving up the mountain.

She looked around. Was she dreaming? Was this real? The young woman was shaken to her core. Nothing like this had ever happened to her. She sat at the bottom of that mountain only minutes ago. It had taken her forty minutes to drive down the mountain and her watch showed only five minutes had passed since she left the patient's home. A stunned Isobel sat for a long time in her car until she felt she could drive to her next patient.

There was no logical explanation for what happened in those few minutes. She sent up a prayer of thanks to God. She knew she had experienced something supernatural.

Eight years passed before she told anyone even her family about the experience. She feared people would think her crazy.

Mountain Path

Isobel says she still cannot shake the feeling that something tragic may have happened on that curvy mountain path had God and his angels not intervened.

Dad's Discipline

I have learned all kinds of things from my mistakes. The one thing I never learn is to stop making them. --- Joe Abercrombie

"Mother, Dad is on the phone," called fifteen-year old Becky answering the phone but never taking her eyes off the snowy fourteen-inch television screen.

The receiver dangling from the wall phone was completely forgotten as Becky's full attention stayed glued to "I Love Lucy," one of her favorite shows. Becky felt privileged with her family being the first in their rural community to own a television set.

Sometime later her mother came into the living room with a worried look, "Your dad is usually home long before now," she said as she looked out the window. "It is getting dark and the rain is still coming down. By the way, why is the phone receiver dandling off the hook?"

"Didn't you talk to Dad?" asked Becky still glued to the television. "He called earlier and I called to you that he was on the phone."

"Well, I didn't hear you," said her mother. She picked up the receiver and hung it in place.

"There's nobody there now. Becky, sometimes I wonder where your mind is."

Just then the door flung open and Becky's dad stomped into the room. He was soaking wet and his face was an awful shade of red. He glared at Becky with a look that could melt steel, walked over and kicked their new television. The set, a floor model, rocked back and forth a few times but didn't turn over.

Anger seemed to be seeping from every pore in his body. Becky jumped up from the chair, ran by her furious dad, and out the door. She felt ashamed. She knew his anger had something to do with her and the phone. It was obvious that her soaking wet dad had walked home in the rain. His car was not outside.

She kept running, paying no attention to the brambles and briars tearing at her skin and clothes. Rain and menacing dark engulfed her. She kept on running until her lungs were a burning mass in her chest. There were no stars to soften the blackness, just the dim moonlight trying to peep through the clouds.

Exhausted, Becky plopped down on a blanket of soft pine needles covering the ground. The faint moonlight showed her to be in the grove of pines behind her house; the thickness of the trees gave some shelter from the rain. She decided to rest for a while and let her dad cool down his anger. She was afraid of the dark but more afraid of going home just yet.

Becky was angry with herself. "Why didn't I make sure Mother answered the phone?" She would have to admit that when she was watching a television program, she was totally oblivious to whatever was going on around her. After answering the phone and calling to her mother, she completely let the phone slip from her mind as she got back into her program. She rushed home from school each day to watch the small snowy face of the new family toy.

After what seemed like hours in the damp cold of the pine grove, Becky knew she could not stay here all night shivering with cold and fear of what awaited her. Slowly, she gathered up her courage and trudged toward home.

Dad's Discipline

The rain had slowed to a drizzle and fog closed in around her like a shroud. She felt an uneasiness that quickened her steps. Becky couldn't remember being wearier both mentally and physically.

The warm glow of lights in the windows seemed to welcome her home. Becky gingerly opened the front door not knowing what to expect. Her mother was sitting in her rocking chair reading a book. She looked up at Becky with relief in her eyes.

"Where were you? I called and called and you didn't answer," said her mother with a look of concern on her face.

"Where is Dad? I'm so sorry about the phone. He's really angry with me, isn't he? He probably wants to kill me." Becky blurted out with remorse in her voice.

"Your dad has gone to bed. He is not going to kill you although he may want to after what you did to him. We're both angry with you. The car stalled and your dad walked to a house to call me to come and get him. He walked home through the rain."

"Why didn't those people bring him home?"

"They didn't have a vehicle available. You know that is the only other house on our lane. Your dad walked half-mile in the rain to get home. Now get out of those wet clothes, go to bed and think about what your punishment ought to be," said her mother sternly.

Becky had a difficult time getting to sleep. Come morning she would have to face her dad. She was already on his stupid list. At breakfast this morning, he asked her to pour him a cup of coffee without spilling it all over him as had happened in the past. Sure enough, she splashed coffee onto his clean white shirt.

He shook his head and left the table to get a clean shirt. He lectured her again about paying attention. Now her inattention had hurt her dad and she was profoundly sorry. Morning dawned bright and clear. Becky's mother called her to get up and get ready for school.

Becky dressed and walked into the kitchen not knowing what she faced. She knew she deserved whatever punishment her dad chose to give her. He was seated at the table; her mother stood at the stove. Nobody spoke. He did not even look at her. They ate breakfast in total silence.

Becky ate quickly, grabbed her books and ran for the bus. She didn't even mind the half-mile walk to the bus stop. Her dad usually dropped her at school on his way to work. No way was she riding with him today. He passed her in the car but did not look her way. She wished he'd yell at her or something. His pretending that she didn't exist was painful.

As the days passed, neither parent mentioned the incident and Becky was glad her dad didn't get rid of the television as he had threatened. Things gradually got back to normal and her dad was talking to her again.

Bad luck raised its ugly head a few weeks later. Becky was learning to drive. Occasionally when she got in from school, her mother would let her back the car in and out of the garage.

"Mother, may I practice with the car if I promise to be careful?" asked Becky with hope in her voice.

"I guess," answered her mother, "but do be careful."

Becky grabbed the keys from the wall key holder and made her way to the garage. She started the motor and mistakenly put the car in drive rather than reverse. Crunch! Oops, she must have rolled over something.

"I hope it's nothing important," Becky said as she got out of the car.

"Oh no! Oh no! It can't be! It just can't be!" cried Becky. She had crushed the new lawn mower her dad had purchased the week before.

It had only been a few weeks since the telephone incident. Dad will really kill me this time. I'm done for," moaned the terror stricken young girl.

This could not be happening, thought Becky, as she sought refuge in her room. In all her fifteen years, she had never felt so depressed and scared.

Dad's Discipline

She heard her dad's car. He was home from work. Her first thought was to run and hide, but she'd have to come out eventually. She peeked out the window and her dad was removing something from the trunk of the car that looked like a sack of fertilizer or grass seed and carrying it into the garage. He didn't come out for several minutes.

Out of the garage came her dad carrying the broken lawn mower. He threw it in the trunk of the car, jumped in the car and sped off. A short time later he was back and stomped into the house.

"Has Becky been practicing with your car?" asked her dad with anger and frustration in his voice.

"Yes, she has. Why?" asked her mother.

That girl ran over the new lawn mower. I took it to the dump. Don't ever let that girl near the car again. She is a menace. She flattened that lawn mower like a pancake. What is the matter with her?"

Becky held her breath as she waited for her dad to come down the hall. The waiting was agony. Where was he? After a while, she breathed a little easier. Eventually her mother called her to supper.

"I'm doing homework. I'm not hungry right now."

No way was she going into the kitchen where her parents were having supper. Days passed and her dad never disciplined her nor mentioned the incident.

Becky could never understand why her dad let the telephone and the lawn mower incidents slide, yet disciplined her for other things.

After thinking about it, she believes either it was because he was so angry he was afraid he might over react, or he just let her live with the agony of waiting and wondering what her punishment would be. I think he knew the agony of wondering when and what he was going to do would be punishment enough. He was right.

The Soup Bean Kettle

Deal with the faults of others as gently as with you own. ---Confucius

Earl and Elmer sauntered up to the general store leading Molly, their old pack mule. They tied her to a post and stepped onto the porch that stretched across the store front. They swapped greetings with some old geezers who were relaxing on wooden benches rolling up their Prince Albert tobacco cigarettes and telling war stories.

The general store built of rough lumber and painted the color of redwood was a focal point in the mountain community. Benches lined the front porch, and inside the store, chairs sat near an old pot-bellied stove. The store offered a little bit of everything from store-bought clothes and groceries to farm supplies. Most folks liked to sit a spell and catch up on the local gossip before buying their supplies.

"Howdy, boys," said Walter, getting up from a bench and following the brothers into the store. "What can I do for you folks today?"

"Ma said to git some coffee, salt and a case of them Pepsi colas," said Elmer.

Walter busied himself getting the needed items and couldn't help but notice how forlorn Earl looked. "You look downcast, Earl. Something bothering you? Are things all right on the mountain?"

"Things ain't too good, Walter. My ma ain't speaking to me. I just don't understand it. I ain't done nothin' wrong. Leastways, I don't think I done wrong but my ma, she thinks I did." Earl said as he plopped down in a chair.

"I'll listen, Earl, if you want to talk about it," Walter said in his jovial friendly way.

"Well, Walter, I think I will talk about it because I want to know if you think I done wrong. It was like this. I had the diarrhea and I couldn't make it to the outhouse. My ma's soup bean kettle was settin on the side table by the stove. I grabbed it and barely had time to git my britches down before out came my business.

"Ma yelled at me awful when she saw what I done. She chased me out of the house with the broom. She said I ruint her kettle. I told her I was sorry and I went right down to the creek and cleaned that kettle. I cleaned that kettle real good. I scoured it out with sand til it shined and then rinsed it in the creek. Now that kettle is as clean as it ever was. Ain't that right, Walter? But Ma didn't think so, and she ain't spoke to me since."

"Well, Earl, I have to say I agree with your ma. You ruined that kettle for sure." Walter said shaking his head and barely hiding his disgust. He realized the idea of cleanliness differed among people, but by any standard this was gross. It was obvious Earl didn't see it that way.

Walter studied the brothers with their scraggly beards, patched bibbed overalls and faded flannel shirts. Nobody would ever accuse them of being overly intelligent so Walter didn't want to judge them harshly. He liked them. The brothers were fiercely loyal to the people they liked and somewhat dangerous to the people they didn't. They usually carried their shotguns with them wherever they went.

The Soup Bean Kettle

Earl and Elmer were probably in their sixties, Walter wasn't sure. They really hadn't changed since he had known them. They could be anywhere from fifty to seventy. Neither of them ever married and they lived with their mother in an isolated log cabin near a mountain creek.

They had no electricity and no indoor facilities even though it was the 1940's. Their water supply came from the creek. They had a cow for milk and a hog to kill in the fall for meat and lard. As with most mountain families, they grew their own vegetables and hunted wild game to supplement their diet. Rabbits, squirrels, deer and wild turkeys were plentiful in the mountains. Blackberries and blueberries grew in abundance.

Walter suspected they had a moonshine still because of the large amounts of sugar they bought. He didn't ask because he didn't want to know. They further supplemented their income selling blueberries and blackberries in season.

Some days later, Walter was having breakfast with his wife. She asked if he'd like a blueberry muffin.

"Those look good. Did you buy the blueberries from Earl and Elmer?" Walter asked

"Yes," his wife replied. "Why?"

"What did they bring them in?"

"They brought them in a kettle. Why do you ask?" said his wife not liking the look on Walter's face.

"I believe I'll pass on the muffins."

"You love blueberry muffins. What's wrong with you?" asked his wife with a puzzled expression.

"I've got something to tell you about Earl and a kettle. By the way, how many of those blueberry muffins did you eat?"

The Taxi

What wisdom can you find that is greater than kindness? --- Jean Jacques Rousseau

The airplane nosed through the clouds and burst forth above the brightly lit airport. Livy heaved a sigh of relief to be at her destination. She felt the fatigue of a long day and a turbulent flight. Her watch showed nine-thirty, as the plane touched down and taxied to a stop. Livy looked forward to getting to her hotel for a hot bath and a warm bed.

Livy's meetings, scheduled for the next day, were located at the university hotel and conference center on the far side of a crime-ridden section of the city. She regretted not booking an earlier flight and getting to the university in daylight. Livy collected her luggage and made her way to the door where taxi drivers were ready to pick up passengers.

The passenger line moved slowly but finally it was Livy's turn for the next taxi. The airport employee assisting people asked Livy for her destination, and then spoke to the driver.

"Sorry, lady, this driver won't go through that section of the city at night," the uniformed worker said as he motioned for the next person in line.

After several cabs refused to take her, Livy began to feel an uneasiness wash over her she recognized as fear. To make matter worse, it began to rain.

"Lady, move over there, please. I'll keep trying to find someone to take you."

Livy felt tears coming. People were looking at her with sympathy but glad her situation was not theirs. The longer Livy stood there, the more fearful she became. Anger and frustration followed fear and then the fear was back again. The hour was getting late, the rain was coming down and Livy had no idea how she was going to get to her hotel. Faith and fear cannot live together in the same mind, so Livy began to pray for God to strengthen her faith that she would find a way out of this dilemma.

An old battered taxi cab moved into position with a matronly looking black woman sitting in the driver's seat. Livy could see she was wearing a house dress in a flowered pattern, the kind her grandmother ordered from the Sears catalog. The woman's round face and dark eyes held a pleasant expression.

The uniformed worker talked with the driver and then turned to Livy and said, "Ma'am, come over here. This driver says she'll take you to your hotel."

Soon her luggage was loaded. If this car had been a race house, it would have been put out to pasture or worse, thought Livy. Beggars can't be choosers, as the old saying goes, so she hopped in without hesitation. When she shut the taxi door, she noticed that it didn't fit properly and wouldn't lock. Much of the material on the inside of the door was pulled away and the seat was well worn with padding sticking out here and there. The car shook and rattled as they pulled away from the curb.

Livy tried talking to the driver to tell her how much she appreciated her courage. She chatted on and on nervously about being a country girl in a strange city on a dark rainy night but the driver never spoke. They were moving along nicely and Livy was

The Taxi

beginning to relax when they came upon a red light in a seedy part of the city.

To the right of the taxi a man was coming toward them with a look on his face that frightened the Livy. He was tall, gaunt, shabbily dressed and wearing a coat much too small for him. His wrists and part of his arms showed below the sleeves. The terrified young woman tried desperately to lock the door to no avail. If the driver was scared, she hid it well.

"Run the red light," Livy wanted to scream.

With great force the man slammed his fist onto the hood of the taxi while muttering something unintelligible. The car shivered and rocked, but before he could make his next move, the light changed and the taxi plunged forward. A thankful Livy gave a great sigh of relief.

They reached Livy's hotel without another incident. She got out of the taxi, paid the driver and gave her a generous tip. In addition to the monetary gift, Livy wanted to give the driver a verbal gift.

"Tonight," the grateful young passenger said, "you have shown who is the more courageous gender. All those male drivers passed me by, but you had the courage to help me. Thank you for your compassion and God bless you!"

The driver still did not speak, but her silence was not filled with attitude, just a quiet confidence. As Livy turned to go, she thanked the woman again and received a smile in response.

Because of that compassionate, courageous woman, Livy did get that hot bathe and warm bed. She never forgot this woman who honored Jesus's example by putting the loving and caring of others into action.

The Vision

There are no mistakes, no coincidences. All events are blessings given to us to learn from." ---Dr. Elisabeth Kubler Ross

It had been a long tiring day and I sank into my bed for a good night's sleep. The clock showed 11:05 p.m. I closed my eyes, snuggled into the covers and there it was---a scene so vivid, I was mesmerized.

Floating near the ceiling in my bedroom was my father. He was dressed in a long, white, flowing garment with a round neckline and long, loose, flowing sleeves. There were gold bands or maybe two brilliant rays of light starting at his shoulders and meeting in a V-shape at his waist.

There were other people dressed the same way milling around who appeared to be pleasantly enjoying themselves. The others were in a mist; not clear and distinct like my dad. There was an expression of peace and contentment on his unlined face; he no longer looked old. His hands were clasped behind his back as he leaned forward and looked down at something he appeared to find interesting. He was not looking toward me. As quickly as the scene came, it was gone. Had it been minutes or only seconds?

The vision was so clear; it was like a movie. Keep in mind that my eyes were closed. This scene was being revealed to me through an inner vision and not with my physical eyes. I screamed and brought my husband out of a deep sleep. He fought his way to consciousness thinking something was terribly wrong.

Trembling and shaking, I told him what I had seen.

He visibly relaxed when he realized there was no tragedy, and told me it was only a dream and to go back to sleep.

I looked at the clock; it showed 11:07 p.m. Only two minutes had passed. Could I have been asleep and dreaming? Too shaken to sleep, I climbed out of bed and went into the living room.

My sixty-year-old dad had died several months earlier of a massive heart attack. The shock of his sudden death left me under a dark cloud of grief that I could not seem to shake. Maybe God allowed me to see how happy and contented my dad was so my grief would lessen.

In the weeks that followed, whenever the scene came to mind, I was comforted and grieving less and less for my dad.

I had not shared my vision with anyone except my husband and my mother. She believed that what I had seen was allowed by God to bring comfort to our grieving family.

Sometime later both my brother and I were visiting our mother. She asked me to tell him about the vision. She thought it might help him handle his grief as it had helped the two of us. After telling him, I noticed a look of astonishment and shock on his face. For a few minutes, he seemed speechless.

After he calmed himself, he told me that he had seen the same scene. He explained that in his mind's eye he saw our dad dressed the same way I had described with the same expression on his face. He said that he was so shaken by his experience that he had yet to tell anyone.

We were stunned that our dad appeared to us both in the same way. We believe God allowed us one last peek at our dad so we could see how happy and contented he was at home in heaven.

Watermelon

"When one has tasted watermelon, one knows what angels eat." --- Mark Twain

A treasured memory from my childhood during the 1950s was slurping cold watermelon in the cool shade of peach trees in my grandparent's yard.

I loved going to their farmhouse, especially on the fourth of July. After the noon meal of fried chicken, green beans, fried potatoes, sliced tomatoes, cucumbers, onions, thick wedges of corn bread, and tall cold glasses of buttermilk, the family relaxed on the front porch. Later in the afternoon the family would go out in the yard for watermelon.

My grandma would toss old patchwork quilts on the grass in the shade of the peach trees, and we would sit down in eager anticipation.

Grandpa would bring from the springhouse a galvanized washtub with a cold watermelon lying inside on a bed of ice. Soon the watermelon juice would be running down chins and elbows, as we relished the huge wedges Grandpa sliced for us.

Angel Wings

Grandma always cautioned us not to eat watermelon before July, because it was "bad for the digestive system," so that first watermelon slice on the fourth of July was a highlight of our summer.

Try as they might, my grandparents could grow almost anything on their farm except watermelons. Before the fourth of July, though, one of the neighboring farmers would drive down to Florida and bring back a truck loaded with the tasty fruit and it door to door.

Grandma would tell Grandpa, "Get a stripped one, Joel, they taste better." He always did.

Those happy years of the 1950s are long gone and my grandparents are in heaven now, but I believe on the fourth of July, my grandma throws an old quilt on a shady, grassy spot in heaven and invites the angels to sit and have a slice of cold watermelon.

White Star Café

It is the sweet, simple things in life, which are the real ones. --- Laura Ingalls Wilder

A sign on the front door delivered its message in black letters "CLOSED". The White Star Café had closed its doors.

Sadness swept over me; the café held many happy memories of my childhood. The White Star Café had been a landmark for over eighty years in our little village town tucked deep in the Cumberland Mountains.

The café was opened following WWI by a soldier home from the army. The veteran could not find a job he wanted, so he decided to open a restaurant. He started with two tables, a counter and four stools. The food was good and the prices reasonable so the little café grew and prospered.

When I began visiting the café in the fifties, it had long outgrown its beginnings and moved to a larger building. The red vinyl covered booths had backs so tall one could stand up and barely see who was in the next booth. They lined one side of the cafe and a long counter with red-vinyl-covered stools lined the other. The cash register was behind the counter near the front door. The owner often stood with his elbow propped on the register and a cigarette in his hand. His hair was glossy black and slicked back with shiny goop. He greeted each customer coming through the door.

One of the large windows on either side of the front door had the words "Plate Lunches" with a white star underneath. The food was nourishing and plentiful. A plate lunch consisted of a meat, two vegetables, corn bread, a dessert and a drink. The cost ran about seventy-five cents. A hamburger was a quarter and a hot dog fifteen cents.

A large multi-colored juke-box with all the latest songs (a nickel a play) sat to the left of the front door. In the mid-1950s, I remember hanging out there after school with my friends and listening to the juke box. Hank Williams was a favorite and Elvis was just coming on the scene. Rock and roll singers and the jitterbug were new and we loved it all.

Through the years when the café was refurbished, the owner kept the décor of the forties and fifties. For me, going in there in later years was like going back in time. Tears came to my eyes when I realized the White Star Café was now only a memory.

In my growing up years, my mom and dad ran a grocery store down the street from the café. When our mom worked late or was tired, she would send my brother and me to the café to eat. We ordered the juicy hamburgers or hot dogs with all the trimmings; not the plate lunches she wanted us to eat.

Hamburgers were a new food for mountain folks in the forties and early fifties. When my grandma came to visit us in town, she had never seen a hamburger, much less tasted one. She asked if they were made out of ham. My brother and I thought our grandma was old-fashioned and funny.

Our family built many memories around the café. We ate there often. I can still recall my dad, who is in heaven now, sitting on one of the red vinyl-covered stools and a waitress serving him a cup of coffee and a piece of pie.

White Star Café

My dad would say, "Bring another piece of that pie, Elziney." He called all waitresses Elziney much to my mom's chagrin.

The café was a gathering place for many of the business people in town, and for people from all walks of life. In later years, when I came home for a visit with my parents, we loved going into the White Star Café, enjoying a good meal, and the décor of an earlier time.

The owner and then his son kept the café opened and serving the people of our small community for over eighty years. The White Star Café may have closed its doors, but the happy memories built around good food and fellowship will not soon be forgotten.

Words Do Hurt

You can forget what hurt you in the past; just never forget what it taught you. --- Anonymous

Nell loved the sport of basketball. Her brother put a basketball in her hands when she was two years old. He turned a kitchen chair upside down and cheered her efforts at shooting goals toward the chair bottom.

She loved it when her parents took her to see her brother play basketball. Twice she slipped away and ran onto the gym floor during a game. Her brother, annoyed and embarrassed, picked up his little sister and carried her to the bleachers.

"Please keep this kid off the court while I'm playing ball," said her brother looking daggers at his parents.

"I was coming to see you, brother," said two-year old Nell.

You must not run on to the gym floor when the game in going on. Those big boys could knock you down and hurt you," said her mom with concern in her voice.

The second time Nell dashed away from her parents and onto the basketball court, they decided attending games with their precocious two-year-old was too risky so they kept her at home.

Angel Wings

"I want to go see my brother play basketball and I want to play on the gym floor," cried Nell when her brother left the house with his gym bag.

A year passed and Nell's parents decided to take their daughter to the games again. "No running onto the court during the game," her mom cautioned her.

The little lady stayed in the bleachers and waited patiently for the game to be over so she could run with the ball up and down the gym floor. Nell would smile and call for her parents to watch her.

Nell excelled at sports from an early age. During seventh and eighth grades, she played on the junior varsity squad. The varsity high school coach saw potential in her and moved the young player to the varsity squad. Nell was only thirteen years old but tall for her age. Coach put the young player on the starting lineup. Some of the varsity players were not happy especially the one whose position she took.

Intimidated by the older players, Nell often sat in the back of the bus by herself. She missed her junior varsity coach and her teammates.

Nell earned many awards through her high school years on the local, district, regional, and state levels. She was selected to the all-state team her junior and senior years. This talented basketball player reached a thousand points her senior year as well as amassing one thousand rebounds. The night Nell scored her thousandth point, the referees stopped the game and presented the ball to her.

Coach said, "Let me have that ball. We are using that for the rest of the game."

"No," said the referee. "It is tradition to give the ball to the player when the thousandth point is reached," and he threw the ball to Nell. "Get another ball for the game," he told the coach.

Nell tossed the ball into the bleachers to her family.

Coach loved attention He would bang his clip board on the scorer's table, jump up and down and scream at the girls and the referees.

"That is his second technical foul. Coach is behaving like a petulant child. Those technical fouls called against him gives the other team opportunities to score points," commented a disgruntled fan during a game.

During game time outs, the spit flew as he yelled at his players. Stupid, lazy, worthless, undeserving of wearing the uniform were some of his favorite comments.

Nell's parents watched their child and her teammates be verbally abused under the guise of what Coach called motivation. He seemed unable to see how his hostile attitude created a negative atmosphere for his team. Nell's mother did go to Coach to talk with him about his behavior. He admitted that he over reacted in the heat of the game and assured Nell's mother that he would do better. He didn't.

Even though Nell was one of the most valuable players on the team, Coach often singled her out and yelled and humiliated her. The first day of practice her senior year, Coach grabbed Nell's jersey and kicked a chair and said to her, "You are lazy, and I am going to tell the college coaches who are recruiting you that you are lazy if you don't step it up." His eyes, face and tone told her he disliked her and she didn't know why. Coach would tell her in private that the game depended on her then undermine her confidence in practice and during the games. Nell felt tremendous pressure from him.

Down through her high school years, the hometown newspapers often put the spotlight on Nell in the sports pages. Some of her teammates were jealous of the attention given to Nell and their comments and attitude toward Nell were hurtful. Often the young player felt she didn't have the support of her team or her coach.

Nell asked her father to approach the reporters at the local paper and request that they tone down the praise. The reporters at the paper were surprised. "Usually people want the attention from us," they said. "We are doing this because we want to help her get a college scholarship. We think she is deserving of the recognition, and we want the colleges to know about her!"

The family appreciated the paper's desire to help but the circumstances on her team made their effort uncomfortable for Nell.

During half time when the players went into the locker room, Coach would often yell at them and put them down. By demeaning them, he replaced self-confidence with self-doubt which can breed jealously, selfishness and mistrust.

Nell graduated and accepted a basketball scholarship to a division two school. The first week of practice, the college coach called her into his office to discuss her on court behavior. He told her he felt she would be a great asset to the team, but he could not understand what he had seen at practice.

"Every time you ran up the floor, you stopped running and looked at me as if I was going to hurt you. If I see something that needs improving. I will tell you when you when you come off the floor. You play your game. What has caused you to have such fear on the court? You looked like a scared little rabbit facing the barrel of a hunter's gun."

"I was waiting for you to yell at me and to tell me how worthless I was and how badly I was playing. I didn't want to be humiliated in front of my teammates."

"You have my word that I will not humiliate you in front of anyone," assured her coach.

Nell loved her college coach because he genuinely cared about the players.

"My teammates and my coach like me, they really like me." Nell told her parents when they came to visit her at the college. "It is awesome."

The young girl learned and grew under the college coach, but it was too late. She no longer loved the game. Nell's negative experience in high school had spoiled the game for her. Even though she cared for her college coach and her teammates, and she felt they cared for her, she could not recover her love of the game. Feeling this way, she didn't believe she would be good for the team. She completed one season, gave up her scholarship and ended her basketball career.

Although Nell graduated from college and went on to get an advanced degree and has been successful in her career, she still carries a residue of hurt from her high school days. Nell learned from her high school experience that emotional abuse can have a lasting effect on a person. Although Nell never became a high school coach, she did coach little league basketball. She strived to bring out the best in the players by encouraging them to have confidence in themselves and to have fun.

When it comes to sports Nell emphatically says, "Too often children and teens are exposed to coaches who forget that sports for children were designed to be healthy physical activities and enjoyable learning experiences."

It is unfortunate that for some coaches the game becomes about their egos and not about the players. They scream, yell, push, humiliate, and even hit children thinking this is the way to motivate. Winning is an admirable goal but not at the cost of abusing children. Coaches are significant adults in the lives of children and can be powerful role models in a negative or positive way.

Society will not allow horses, dogs and other animals to be mistreated but allow kids to be bullied in sports venues all across the country.

Mother's Bucket List

You will never get a cup of tea large enough or a book long enough to suit me.---C. S. Lewis

Joelle, my niece, found these lists among my mother's papers following her death at age ninety.

Many of the items on the list were things Mother did as a small child following at the heels of her grandma as she did her chores on the farm.

Below are the two lists just as Mother wrote them.

Things I Would Like To Experience Again
1. Set a hen (Put eggs under a hen to hatch for little chicks.)
2. Find a hen's nest with new-born chicks
3. See a new foal
4. Cook on a wood stove
5. Plant a garden
6. Get a puppy
7. Ride a horse
8. Walk

9. Go fishing
10. Most of all go to church again. Seems I've lost all that makes life worth living.

Things I Love
1. Rain, the gentle gift from heaven, the good scent of the dry ground as the rain falls.
2. BABIES (The caps were Mother's)
3. Coffee boiling in the morning
4. Ripening of apples in the autumn
5. Chicken frying at supper time.
6. BOOKS
7. Music (some music) a lot that passes for music isn't.
8. Birds
9. Horses – I even like the smell of horses
10. Dogs – all animals. They are an important part of our lives – cows, horses, sheep, etc.
11. Fishing - so long ago since I went fishing. I loved it. Grandma Julie Ann did, too.

Mother ended her list with this sentence, "God has given us so many precious things. Most of the things I have mentioned are lost to me now. I am old and weak but thankful for life as it is."

My mother was born on November 24, 1917, the oldest of eight children. She lived to be ninety years old. Her greatest joy, I think, was her books. She loved to read and she encouraged my love of reading. C. S. Lewis was one of her favorite authors. She quoted from his books often. Mother bought copies of *Mere Christianity* by C. S. Lewis and distributed them to friends and family.

"Make us a cup of tea," my mother would say when I came through the door to visit her.

We would have our tea and she would discuss whatever book she was reading. She read widely. One of her favorite places to go was the library. I remember one day Mother had so many books to carry, the librarian gave us a box. An article appeared in the library newsletter featuring my mother and her love of reading. Mother would pick out an author and if she enjoyed the writing then we would read all or most of his or her books.

Mother loved the book, *Gone with the Wind* by Margaret Mitchell. "Every page in that book is well written," she would say. "Some of the books she encouraged me to read were Tolstoy's *War and Peace,* Ayn Rand's, *Atlas Shrugged,* and *The Confessions of Saint Augustine,* so we could discuss those books." I enjoyed reading but with a full-time job and a family, those thick books were too time-consuming.

When I retired I did read *War and Peace* and *Atlas Shrugged* but at this point I have not read *The Confessions of Saint Augustine* and I probably never will.

When I entered my teen years, I would sneak and read a magazine called *True Romance*. My friend shared her copies with me. One day my dad walked by me and noticed what I was reading.

Do you know what this girl is reading?" called Dad to Mother.

"Yes, I know" my mother said. "She will learn those stories are all the same and she'll become bored with them."

She was right. Mother carefully fostered my love of reading and taught me what pleasure a good book can bring. The joy of reading is one of the greatest gifts my mother gave to me. The first poem I can remember Mother reading to me was Robert Frost's "Stopping by the Woods on a Snowy Evening." My grandpa would encourage me to read by leaving books open to interesting parts so I would see them and be curious.

The contrast between Mother's world as a young girl and mine is mind boggling, especially accessibility of books. The world changed drastically over the course of Mother's ninety years. She often said, "Young people today would find it difficult to imagine living the way I grew up."

One of the most important persons in my mother's life was her Grandma Julie Ann, born in 1877. Mother's love of reading evolved from her relationship with her grandma. I enjoyed hearing Mother tell stories about her.

Mother told about her grandma going into the woods to find a splinter of cedar (sweet wood, her grandma called it) and whittle a crochet hook. Mother said she never knew if there were none available to buy or if her grandma just didn't have the money.

"I helped Grandma Julie Ann make soap," Mother said. "In an iron pot over an outdoor fire, Grandma put water, grease, lye and I don't know what else and cooked it until it looked creamy and started to thicken. Before it stopped cooking, she would put clean washed roots of sassafras to make it smell better. When it cooled she cut it in blocks and laid them on boards to harden. She used that soap for bathing and for cleaning."

Grandma Julie Ann had little formal education but she loved to read. She longed for books.

"During my high school years," Mother said, "Grandma would ask me to bring her books from the school library. I would try to pick out what I thought she'd like because I was a reader, too. We had a scanty little library. There was not much there for a reader; books were precious and difficult to find in Grandma's time. There were no public libraries."

A vivid memory of my mother's love of books happened one crisp fall day when the postman delivered a carton to our home. Mother had ordered the complete works of twelve classical authors such as, Edgar Allen Poe, Shakespeare, Jane Austen, Longfellow, and others. She picked up each book and held it to her heart as if it were a precious gem. My dad was yelling at her that she had spent a whole week's salary on some damn books. Mother was oblivious to what he was saying; his ranting didn't matter because she had her books.

When the first public library opened in our town in 1958, Mother was elated. She had longed for this for so many years and finally it happened. The library was her favorite place to go while she was on earth.

Now that she is in heaven I like to think of Mother sitting in a rocking chair in a beautiful library with all the greatest books ever written all around her, perfect eyesight and all eternity to read. Who knows, she may also be doing things from her bucket list.

Blackberries and Buttermilk

"A bird in the hand is a certainty, but a bird in the bush may sing for you."
Bret Hart

"Well, John, I fixed my own supper tonight. Lizzy ain't feelin' good. She took her bed."

"What did you fix, Ben?"

"Blackberries and cold buttermilk. I do like juicy ripe blackberries. Lizzy keeps plenty of cold buttermilk and sweet milk in the springhouse. That's good eating -- a glass of cold buttermilk and a bowl a blackberries covered with sweet milk and honey," said Ben as he patted his stomach.

The old friends were genuinely enjoying each other's company on this cool late summer night. Ben picked up his banjo and began strumming easily as he chatted with his old friend.

"Ben, folks around here sure do like listening to you and Bob play your music. Your son can really play that fiddle. You two are in great demand for the pie suppers and barn dances around here."

"Yep, and we enjoy playing. I think we get on Lizzy's nerves. At the end of the day Lizzy likes to sit quiet and read her Bible but me and Bob like to play a little music."

Speaking of Lizzy, I hear she build your new barn. Is that a fact?"

"She did, John. I helped her some, but Lizzy is better at building things than I am. She builds and repairs fences right along with me," boasted Ben. "There ain't much Lizzy can't do."

Darkness was enfolding the two men as they sat and talked companionably together long into the evening.

"I'm going to mosey on home, Ben," said John getting up from his chair. Ben stood, stretched his six feet, five inch frame, picked up his banjo and went inside. There was a chill in the night air and the fire in the fireplace felt good. He relaxed in his rocker, picked up his knife and a piece of wood and began to whittle.

One of Ben's favorite pastimes was whittling. His grandchildren loved the interesting objects that took shape from the wood in his gnarled work-worn hands – maybe a bird, a flower or an animal. He often sang as he whittled. The song about going fishing in a crawdad hole was one of the children's favorites.

The grandchildren loved Grandpa Ben. They especially loved it when he got out his banjo or fiddle and played for them. They grasped their whittled treasures and danced around the room to the happy tunes.

Ben's talents didn't fit the life he lived. He could sing, play the banjo and the fiddle. He could make wood come alive in his hands, but when it came to things like farming and barn building, he was lacking. When his music playing and wood working got in the way of chores that needed doing, Ben reminded himself that he was a dirt farmer with a wife and six kids to support.

Lizzy would shake her head at yet another crooked furrow, or fence-mending fiasco, but her affection for Ben was genuine, so she made allowances. If the family needed a barn or a fence, she could do the job. Her farming skills were more than competent, too.

Blackberries and Buttermilk

Lizzy's hands were constantly busy whether quilting for her family, helping to raise their food, or sewing their clothes. She also understood her husband's need to play his music and work with wood, so she tolerated the wood chips on the floor and the frequent visits of family and friends because as one child put it, "It is so fun at Grandpa Ben's house."

Ben and his son, Bob, were always in demand to play the fiddle and banjo for pie suppers, barn dances and other community socials. Ben enjoyed social gatherings; not so for Lizzy. She loved sitting quietly with her crocheting, quilt making, or tatting lace.

Lizzy was an ample woman, nearly six-foot tall, big boned but slender with kind brown eyes and dark blond hair pulled into a bun at the back of her head. Her dresses were ankle length with high necks, long sleeves and covered in front with a long white apron tied at her waist. Whether she was working in the fields, the garden, or the house, she dressed the same.

Life for Ben and Lizzy held none of the material things that are considered essential today. Their log home had no electricity, no indoor plumbing, no central heating, no technological gadgets and they raised their own food. They had their faith, the changing seasons, each other, and their children. There was a huge fireplace for warmth, cooking, and sitting around on a cold winter's night.

In the late winter of their lives many, many years ago in a much simpler time, Ben and Lizzy enjoyed their front porch where they smoked their pipes and rocked in their cane bottom rockers. Arthritis and old age stole from Ben his whittling and wood working, and Lizzy's heart problems kept her limited to light household tasks. Lizzy continued to enjoy making quilts and crocheting.

Ben still strummed the banjo and one of his favorite meals continued to be a bowl of fresh blackberries with milk and honey and a glass of cold buttermilk.

The Dream

Never make the blunder of trying to forecast the way God is going to answer your prayer.---
Oswald Chambers

"Please let him come to me in a dream. Father God, let me see and talk to him one more time," I prayed. On my knees by the bed I continued to pray fervently. With tears in my eyes, I crawled into bed believing this would be the night I would dream of my husband, Harold.

I lost my husband to cancer after fifty-two years of marriage. I missed him terribly. Some people say they dream of their loved ones soon after they leave this earth. Why was this not happening for me? Tonight instead of wishing for my husband to come to me in a dream, I prayed on my knees for it to happen.

The dream God gave me that night is still vivid in my mind. I will never forget it. I dreamed that Harold was walking toward me. He had on a dark suit with a white shirt and dark tie. This was unusual attire for him because in life he preferred light blues, tans and grays for his sport coats and suits. His shirts were light colors or muted stripes. These were the kind of clothes he wore in his job as a school administrator. To see him in black was somewhat disconcerting. He appeared to be dressed for a formal affair.

He looked wonderful and I ran to him screaming with tears of joy running down my cheeks, "You came! You came! God answered my prayer."

I pulled him into my arms and he was solid and strong. The fabric of his coat felt like regular suit material as my fingers brushed his back. He was not at all mist-like. He looked young and there was no gray in his hair.

My excitement built as I blurted out how wonderful to see him and that I had a million questions to ask. As I pulled back to look at him, I noticed he was not happy with me and I could not understand his reaction. His arms were by his side and he did not put them around me. He did not look at me but rather looked straight ahead. I was so happy to see him I did not immediately react to his serious demeanor.

"Will you answer some questions for me?" I asked with my enthusiasm still at high pitch.

The questions poured forth from me and he answered them all never looking at me rather continuing to look straight ahead. I remember thinking; I am going to remember every word he is saying. I was confused about his attitude but was so happy to be with him I did not let that curb my joy.

One of my questions was about heaven and if it was as beautiful as we think; he said yes. That is the only question and answer I can remember. The other questions I asked and the answers he gave have been erased completely from my mind. Maybe God answered my prayer and sent Harold to me and let us say whatever we wanted and then He decided what I would remember and erased the rest.

My husband's attitude of aloofness left me hurt and confused. As marriages go, ours was among the best. We loved and respected each other and raised our kids in a loving Christian home. I thought he ought to be as happy to see me as I was to see him.

The Dream

"I don't understand your behavior," I said.

While he did not speak as he did when answering my questions, I seemed to be able to understand his thoughts. "Don't do this again. Do not call me back. I cannot come where you are, and it is not the time for you to come through this door." He started walking toward a metal door that appeared before us. There were other people standing around the door but I did not recognize any of them.

Then the strangest thing happened. He turned and looked right at me for the first time and I saw sadness for me in his eyes. I sensed strongly he wanted me to let him go and to stop holding on to my grief. Maybe, I thought, he would not look at me earlier because he didn't want me to see his eyes. Could it be that grief can be so intense as to reach across time and space and be felt by those who have transitioned into heaven? Maybe that was the reason for the black suit and tie, to help me see him in a different way.

Harold walked through the metal door made of open panels and each panel began to slam shut. As the last panel closed, I was left standing there alone.

I awakened with a start feeling somewhat confused. Even though it was only a dream, it felt so real. The feel of his suit coat material still lingered on my fingers. I will never forget how young and strong he looked and felt to me.

Three years have passed since my husband made the transition to heaven. I have never again prayed for God to send him to me in a dream and I never will. My prayer was a selfish one. Failure to let go of our loved ones in our hearts and minds may keep them from embracing all the glories of heaven.

Made in the USA
Charleston, SC
13 February 2015